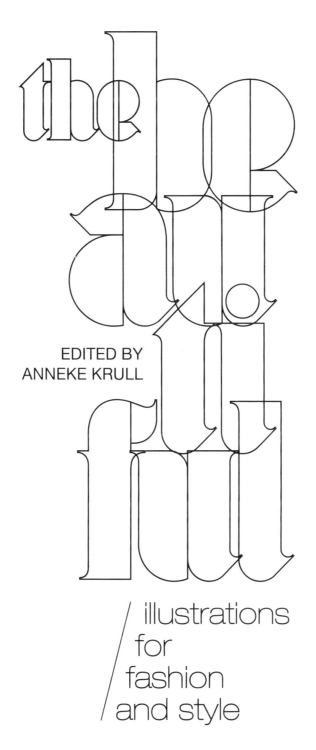

the beautiful

EDITED BY
ANNEKE KRULL

/ illustrations
/ for
/ fashion
/ and style

gestalten

minihava•s

Combine a love for fashion, colors, and art, shake them all up, and you'll get Finnish illustrator Minni Havas' body of work. Mixing traditional drawing skills with modern imagery, the illustrator creates drawings with water-soluble color pencils before giving them a finishing touch with a few clicks of the mouse and the computer. She is based in Helsinki and represented by Agent Pekka.

1. CANCER, 2010, Anorlang – The Face. 2. FUR HAT, 2009, Personal. 3. CUPCAKES, 2009, Marketing – Free State. 4. CELLO, 2009, Personal. 5. COVER ARTWORK, 2010, Babyal – IWD magazine.

tina berning

By the time Tina Berning was 11 years old, snipping out pictures from newspaper supplements and pasting them onto walls, she already knew she wanted to become an illustrator. Now in her adult years, she explores the topic of women who are graceful, but whose beauty remains unfinished. – She typically works on beautiful old paper found in flea markets and old books. She is the author of 100 Girls on Cheap Paper, and has contributed to the New York Times, Cosmopolitan, Architectural Digest, Playboy, Emotion, and more.

1. TATTOO, 2010. *Editorial* – Playboy, U.S. 2. BIOGRAPHY, 2009.
Editorial – Vita. 3. LEO, 2009. *Editorial* – Cosmopolitan.
4. CATHY AUGENBLICK, 2010. *Editorial* – Playboy, U.S. 5. AQUARIUS,
2009. *Editorial* – Cosmopolitan.

LULU gathered her first impressions of form and color in her mother's flower shop in Solingen, Germany, where she was born in 1977. This early inspiration is still visible in some of her fashion illustration work, while her other work refers to computer graphics or retro aesthetics. She graduated best in her class with a degree in design from the Cologne International School of Design in 2002 and worked in San Franciscan design firm Futurefarmers and Swiss design office Buero Destruct, before focusing on her work as an illustrator. She has lived in Berlin since 2003.

sti
na
Pers
son

1. REFINED, 2010. Exhibition – Galeri Karlshov 2. MEN FASHION, 2010. Exhibition – Galeri Karlshov 3. BIG HAIR, 2010. Exhibition – Galeri Naples 4. CADHABAY, 2010. Exhibition – Galeri Karlshov 5. STRAWBERRI BLONDE, 2010. Exhibition – Galeri Karlshov

Stina Persson's preferred media of ink, watercolor, and gouache on Mexican cut paper enhance the fluidity of her lines, which flow onto the paper. She fuses the traditional with the edgy to introduce a modern look to illustration – a look that is appreciated by numerous clients, including Lilet and Macy's department stores. Persson studied fine art in Umbria, fashion drawing in Florence, and also has a degree in Illustration from Pratt Institute in New York. In 1996 and 1997, she was awarded the Society of Illustrators Student Scholarship, and has exhibited her work in several shows in New York and Japan.

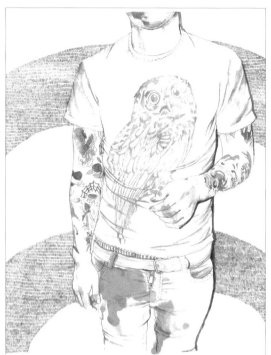

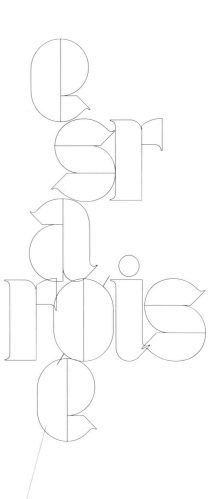

esra rose

Esra Rose started out as an illustrator with two years at Einar Granum School of Arts, and is currently studying for her bachelor's degree in visual communication at the National Academy of Arts in Oslo, Norway. Her contemporary graphic work has been featured at the Somerset House in London, and in Nylon, Vixen Magazine, and A Doll's House, a fanzine Rose started with several of her friends. She is represented by HigginsonHurst Agency in London.

1. NOW IS THE ONLY TIME I KNOW, 2010, Personal
2. SWIGGS, 2009, Fanzine - Rise Festival 3. THE BIRTHDAY PARTY, 2009, Personal 4. SCREAM & ICE CREAM, 2010, Personal
5. UNTITLED, 2010, Fanzine - A Doll's House Style 6. STRIPES, 2010, Personal 7. FLOWERS, 2009, Personal

christina drejenstam

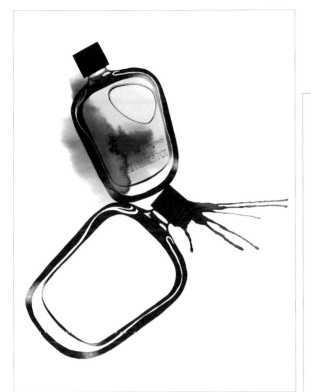

cassandra rhodin

1. BEAR, 2009. *Personal.* 2. HYENA, 2009. *Personal.*
3. LEOPARD, 2009. *Personal.* 4. BIRD, 2009. *Personal.*
5. GORILLA, 2009. *Personal.* 6. ICE BEAR, 2009. *Personal.*

With five generations of artists behind her, it was only natural that Cassandra Rhodin could perform magic with paper and pen, illustrating for the likes of H&M, Nylon, Urban Outfitters, Elle, and Stockholm's East restaurant. Her inspiration of luxe cabaret glamour from Paris in the 1920s can be seen in her work. She has a distinct fondness for carnivals and magnificent animal kingdoms – the sort in which her great grandfather, circus king Brazil Jack, thrived. Rhodin also has a clothing line of fashionable childrenswear Mini Rodini, which she founded in 2006.

nadia flower

As her name implies, Nadia Flower concerns herself with all things delicate and fragile, and where daydreams meet fantasy. Each of her illustrations wields a strong visual message topped with a feminine twist. Combining hand-drawn and computer-based imagery with delicate lines, the artist produces illustrations and textile designs for clothing labels, magazines, and advertisements. Her clients include Lily Allen, Fornarina, Nylon, ghd, Coca-Cola (UK), British Glamour, Saatchi & Saatchi, Yen Magazine, Grazia, David Jones, and Zoe and Morgan.

1. RUN IN THE DARK, 2009, Personal.
2. WILD AT HEART, 2009, Personal.
3. FLIRTING, 2008, Personal. 4. BUILT IN A DAY, 2009, Personal. 5. MY LITTLE PONY, 2009, Personal.

CRYING OUT

my dead a pony

RAWBOWS

Illustrator mydeadpony (a.k.a. Rachael Vicanzi) lives in Brussels, Belgium, with his wife and daughter. He is represented by the Colagene agency.

i pushed MYSELF
SO

HARD▶

that my skull POPPED OUT

I think i've lost my emotions

daniel egnéus

For Daniel Egnéus, born in 1972 in Sweden, everyday life and art are one inseparable whole: his Milan and Rome surroundings, his friends and girlfriend, and last but not least his day-dreaming, constantly find a way into his work. Egnéus has lived and worked in Milan for ten years. He has no formal education.

Swedish illustrator Cecilia Carlstedt knew early on what her career path would be. After studying at the London College of Printing and The Fashion Institute of Technology in New York, she quickly went on to provide her sophisticated brand of illustrations for La Perla, the New York Times, H&M, and Swarovski. Her preferred media is a mix of traditional mediums like pencil and ink in combination with modern techniques including Illustrator, Photoshop, and photography. Carlstedt counts Elisabeth Peyton, Marlene Dumas, and Gerhard Richter among her main artistic influences.

1. SKETCH FASHION, 2009. Self-initiated – Personal 2. VOGUE NDA, 2009. Editorial – Vogue india 3. UNTITLED, 2008. T-shirt print – dessigns 4. JUDITH, 2008. Print for sale – Wonderalice 5. JUDITH ED, 2010. Cover editorial – Crecilia magazine

spiros halaris

Greek artist Spiros Halaris has been in the design industry for several years and is exploring new types and styles of visual communication. She would like to work for fashion houses and magazines around the globe. As an illustrator, she likes to challenge herself and continually break new ground. Black tones play a prominent role in the Athens-based artist's work, a sharp contrast to the detailed intricacy of the hand-drawn illustrations.

1. FEATHER DAY, 2009, Editorial – Personal 2. WINTER TIME, 2009, Editorial – Personal 3. IN HER DRESS, 2009, Editorial – Personal 4. GIRL WITH ONE EYE, 2009, Editorial – Personal 5. COMPLICATED, 2009, Editorial – Personal

naja conrad-hansen

Naja Conrad-Hansen's practice embraces illustration, painting, graphic design, art direction, and silk-screen prints. The half-Finnish, half-Dane's work has been included in a number of fashion and graphic design publications. She also designs prints and patterns for various clothing labels, including a limited-edition print for her own brand. Meannorth Conrad-Hansen was nominated and selected for 200 Best Illustrators Worldwide by Lürzer's Archive for 2007–2008 and again in 2009–2010. She is a graduate of Denmark's Design School with an MA in Visual Communication and a background in fine art.

1. CIGAR BOX BEAUTY. 2010. Exhibition – Miss Scarlet in the Field.
2. CIGAR BOX BEAUTY. 2010. Exhibition – Miss Scarlet in the Field.
3. CIGAR BOX BEAUTY. 2010. Exhibition – Miss Scarlet in the Field.
4. LIR. 2009. Editorial & UNTITLED. 2010. Exhibition – Green Number.

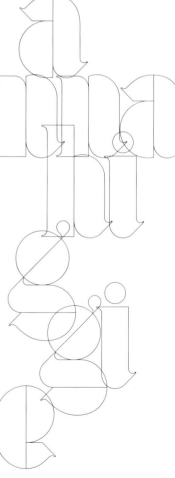

anna higgie

Based in Barcelona, Anna Higgie is an artist and illustrator with a penchant for drawing graphic and edgy portraits of fashion's familiar faces. Her work has been featured in Crush/Cookies Berlin, Dazed and Confused, Don't Panic, Essence, the Guardian, and Icon. Among other things, she has a passion for photography and food, which she exhibits on her personal blog.

1. DIAMANDA GALLAS 2008. Editorial. Plan B magazine
2. STAM 2010. Personal 3. VANJA 2008. Personal 4. UNTITLED 2008. Personal 5. THERE 2008. Self-promotion—Art Department

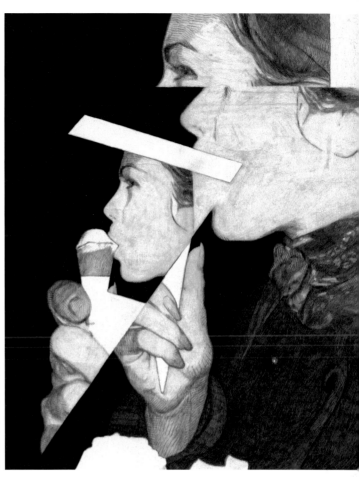

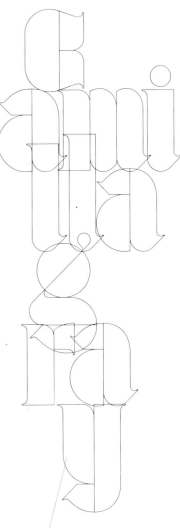

No job could be more perfect for 28-year old Brazilian artist Camilla Gray than being a fashion illustrator. Illustration and fashion are her passions. The Brazilian artist creates drawings by hand with a mechanical pencil, then scans and manipulates them with watercolor splashes and photoshopped textures and pops of color. The result is illustrations that smack of dreamy femininity and precision at once. Gray's work often features famous figures in the industry, such as model Jessica Stam or the late Alexander McQueen.

1. EPIC, Watercolor, 2010. Personal. 2. BATMAN, 2009. Personal. 3. BOHEME, 2008. Personal. 4. TYRA, Ink, 2009. Personal. 5. ALEXANDER, 2010. Personal. 6. SHE DEVIL, 2008. Personal.

amelie ghebart

Amelie Hegardt, an illustrator from Stockholm, is represented by Traffic NYC in the
United States and Darling Management in Sweden. Her colorful watercolor
paintings often feature drippy, bleeding ink elements that lend the illustrations a sense
of whimsy and spontaneity.

1 UNTITLED, 2009, Editorial: Exhibit – S Magazine
2 UNTITLED, 2009, Editorial – Pascual
3 UNTITLED, 2009, Editorial: Exhibit – S Magazine
4 SQUARES, 2010, Editorial – Cameron, Jurd Magazine
5 UNTITLED, 2008, Editorial: Exhibit – S Magazine

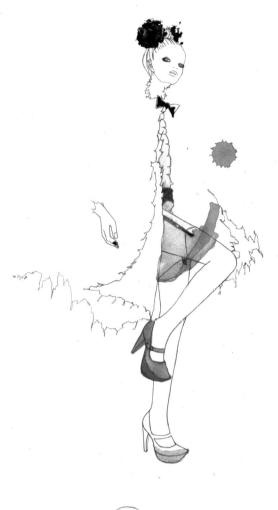

micca

1. ZAC2, 2009, Resona 2, FFD, 2010,
Bookcover – SDP, 3. ZAC3, 2009, Firewall
4. CXMM, 2009, Resona 5, 1C8, ZC, 2009,
Shop card – Maïya

Japanese illustrator Micca was born in 1976 in Mie Prefecture, Japan. She graduated
in 1998 from Kyoto Seika Art University and her work is typically characterized as
simple line drawings on pink matte paper with an occasional pop of color. She favors
capturing women caught in the middle mundane tasks. Micca's work can also
be found on magazine covers, CD jackets, and web sites. She has also worked in
collaboration with a number of fashion brands.

bendour

1. SPRAY 2, 2009 Exhibition – Maha Gallery, Toronto
2. MODEL SKETCH, 2010, Personal 3. SPRAY 3, 2009
Exhibition – Maha Gallery, Toronto 4. QUEEN SKETCH, 2009
Personal 5. INT. LIFE SKETCHES, 2010, Exhibition – Maha Gallery,
Vancouver 6. GUILD 1, 2009, Exhibition – Joshua Liner Gallery, N.Y.C

Based in Vancouver, B.C., painter and illustrator Ben Tour has shown his work in Los Angeles,
Miami, New York City, and Hamburg. His illustrations have been featured in lifestyle
publications including Playboy, Juxtapoz, and Color Magazine. Clients with a decidedly
masculine slant include such as BMW, Absolut, and Nike Snowboarding.

carine brancowitz

French illustrator Carine Brancowitz works from the most basic of tools – the ballpoint pen – to push boundaries where others might only find limitations. Imagine one spectacular doodle from middle school and you have the result: illustrations that combine the purity and passion of adolescent anxiety, an obsessive attention to detail, an uncluttered elegance of lines, and a compositional severity. Her work has been featured on graphic t-shirts and in publications such as French Cosmopolitan, Nylon, De Zeit, Arena, and Italian Vogue Pelle.

1. ESCALATOR, 2009, Personal 2. DIPTYQUE 1, 2010, Personal 3. DIPTYQUE 2, 2010, Personal 4. RACCOON'S, 2008, Personal 5. STYLE, 2009, T-shirt print—Pig.Soil

carmen garcía huerta

1 VANESSA, 2010 Recent solo exhibition – BACI Festival
Pandora's Box edition 10, MU, MU, PINK CONNECTION, 2010
Finalist 3 EUROGRAFICS PRIZE 2010 Illustration over
Marie Madame I LAURA 2009 Recent group exhibition
art Piction – Pifdong's Box editions 1,2,3,1,2,3, 78-78 Helsinki
© BIO, MARS 2009, Finland

After graduating with a degree in advertising, Madrid based artist Carmen García Huerta started her career as a
graphic designer. She found her true calling as a fashion illustrator in 2001 after achieving immediate success
working for Spanish publications like Elle, Woman, Vogue, El País Semanal and Vanidad. She later expanded her
clientele list to a broad range of international clients, including French companies like Eric Bompard, Nivea,
Glamour Germany, and RaU Japan. She has recently developed a more personal, less polished style, which
was showcased at the BACI Festival 10 Pandora's Box in Barcelona last December.

brettmanning

Besides coffee, chocolate, cats, and 1960s tunes, Chicago-based illustrator Brett Manning counts art as one of his top loves. He explores the theme of man-made versus natural in his work, which he expresses through an abundance of texture, balance, pattern, fashion, and femininity. The result is a series of surreal and dream-like illustrations that have been featured in Juxtapoz, Mt Magazine, Cheap Magazine, and a number of gallery shows in Chicago, Los Angeles, and Ottawa, Ontario.

carmen segovia

Carmen Segovia was born in Barcelona, Spain in 1978. After studying cinema and theater, she concentrated solely on painting and illustration. Today she contributes to prestigious newspapers and agencies, illustrates for international publishers, and collaborates with bands on music projects. Her work as an illustrator and author has been awarded internationally and has been featured in Society of Illustrators 49, American Illustration 27, Workbook, and Bologna Fiction Annual.

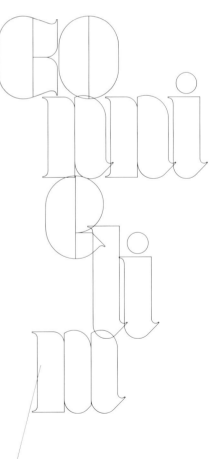

Conni Glim

natalia czajkiewicz

Natalia Czajkiewicz is an artist living and working in Seattle, Washington. Raised in California, she creates work heavily influenced by her sun-soaked youth and the gray contrast of the Pacific Northwest. Nostalgic and sentimental, she is inspired by women, human interaction, internal alarms, and hand-drawn type.

1. THINKING ABOUT LOVE, 2008. Personal
2. STRETCHING, Personal. 3. IN OUR COVER, 2008.
Personal. 4. I'LL CALL OUT FOR YOU SOMETIMES.
2008. Personal. 5. THE BLUES, 2009. Personal

lahel kovacs

1 OXI_2008 Editorial – The Room Magazine 2 ANTLOFF 2008
Editorial – The Room Magazine 3 FISH 2008 The Room Magazine
4 SHEH 2008 Editorial – The Room Magazine 5 OH-MAMA 2008
Editorial – The Room Magazine PANDA 2008 Editorial – The Room Magazine

With a window-dressing degree and a graphic design past, Budapest-based artist
Lahel Kovács could only create bold, joyful illustrations meant to catch the eye.
His hand-drawn works are usually combined with digitally created colors, and convey
a certain sense of joy. The artist also makes screen prints.

denise van leeuwen

Born in 1981 in the Netherlands, Denise van Leeuwen stems from a creative family that nurtured her passion for drawing at an early age. She works with pen and pencil, mostly graphite, and features those close around her in her illustrations: friends, family and, occasionally, herself. Among her inspirations she names 1960s advertisements, Alfons Mucha, fashion and typography. Her work has been featured in books such as Illusive 2, Illusive 3 and The Sourcebook of Contemporary Illustration

REWARD !, 2008. Editorial – BEAUTY. SQUARED, 2009. Editorial – Leichzeichen (ZEIT), 2008. Editorial – Adelaide (ELLE), 2010. Editorial – Lucky RAINE, 2009. Illustration 5 OLOG, 2008. Editorial – Avantgarde AO 1

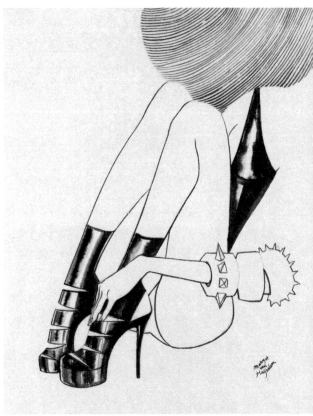

margot van huijkelom

margot
mace

There is something a little off, a little sinister, in Parisian artist Margot Mace's illustrations – and
that is exactly what makes her work popular among Vogue Japan, Madame Figaro, Clarins, Lancôme,
and Biotherm clients, among others. Using watercolors, ink pen, Japanese brush, paper, and oil
paints, the artist creates wonderfully fragile and expressive illustrations that have also been featured
in the Gestalten books Illusive 1 and Illusive 2.

1. COCO GIRLS, 2009. Editorial – Soon magazine.
2. QUIETE, 2009. Editorial – Soon magazine. 3. COWGIRL,
2009. Editorial – Soon magazine. 4. COCO JEANS, 2009.
Editorial – Soon magazine. 5. MASCARA, 2009. Clarins.

caitlin shearer

Ciatlin Shearer '09

1. GILDED MIRROR, 2009. Personal 2. HOPE FSS, 2009. Advertising – Hopeless Lingerie 3. CARDBOARD CLOUDS, 2009. Personal 4. MAIDEN VOYAGE, 2010. Personal 5. POLKA DOTTED, 2009. Personal 6. BRASSERIE, 2009. Personal

Twenty-year-old fine artist and illustrator Caitlin Shearer hails from the seaside of New South Wales, Australia. Her work reflects a distinct passion for the golden years of Hollywood, all things vintage, and Fred Astaire. Shearer enjoys rendering imaginary people in watercolors, pencil, and fine vintage dresses.

Cabri
stinak

1. IN THREADS, 2008, Exhibition piece – Dance Dot Gallery
2. IgNiS, 2009, Peace 3, CA22, 2010, Coffey – Insight51
4. ATHENA, 2008, Personal 5, 60.00, UK Still, 2009, Personal
© Black – 2009, Coffey – Something Else

Illustrator, designer, screen printer, film lover – call her what you will but Christina K is an artist of many dimensions. She utilizes traditional and digital mark making techniques to impose a subtle narrative in her drawings, which appear at once striking and delicate. She has worked with such clients as Ogilvy & Mather, Levis, La Perla, Chanel, Bloomingdales, and Hintmag. Her illustrations have been featured in a host of books, including Fashion Wonderland, At Allure, and 9 Sushi.

The work of artist and fashion illustrator Erin Petson can most accurately be described as delicate, sensual and ethereal. She uses textures and marks to create unique and stunning imagery. Her figurative drawings explore fashion with abstract elements. Petson studied illustration in Liverpool and now resides in East London, although her clients span an international range such as Vogue Nippon, Brizo, Lancôme, Selfridges, and the New York Times. Her work has been exhibited across the world, from Los Angeles to Paris to Tokyo.

1. TIGER GIRL. 2009. Fashion print – solo label. 2. TART GIRL. 2009. Exhibition Show – 'Ferocious'. 3. ELVA. 2010. Exhibition Show – 'Ferocious'. 4. BONDELLE. 2009. Editorial fashion illustration – ST Magazine. 5. EADU. 2009. Exhibition Show – 'Ferocious'. 6. CHLOE. 2009. Editorial fashion illustration – ST Magazine.

fontaine anderson

Fontaine Anderson studied visual communications at The University of South Australia and illustration at Parsons, New York. She has worked for clients such as Anna Sui, Visa, Element, Topshop, Something by Natalie Wood Hurley, Penguin, the Guardian, Fader, and Bust magazine. She currently lives and works in London.

1. STALE, 2009, Fashion graphics—Element 2. DAPHNE, 2009, Personal 3. GRAFIC LADY, 2007, Bust magazine, SLEEPWALKER, 2004, Personal 4. BLER, 2008, Fashion graphic—Anna Sui 5. GIRL POWER, 2009, Personal

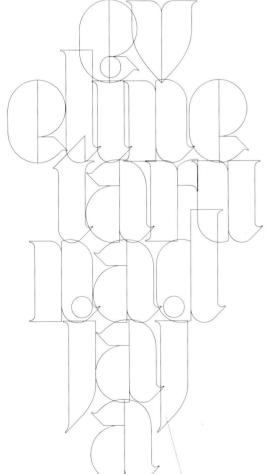

1. and 2. UNTITLED, 2006. Drawing. 3. FLUORITH, 2006.
Personal. 3. HOURGLASS, 2006. Personal. 4. PLAIN PLACE, 2006.
Personal. 5. PAGAN SETTS, 2006. Personal.

Eveline Tarunadjaja's current work is recognizable by the intricate detail of the cascading hair she illustrates.
The Australian-based artist is fueled by a passion for stories, Asian customs, guilty pleasures, and octopi, and
she saturates her drawings with a self-described "sugary and mischievous imagery." Among others,
Tarunadjaja has been featured in publications such as Vogue Girl Korea, Frankie (Australia), and Crafuck 3
(U.S.A.), and has designed art for fashion labels such as Hurley, Billabong, Gorman, Anna Sui, and
French Kitty. She has also designed one-off CD and book covers for Shock Records and Penguin.

lisabil
l o
vik

Swedish illustrator and fashion designer Lisa Billvik works with illustration in different contexts: on commission and within her own projects. Her work typically shows the consumption of fashion and clothing, combining a feeling of discretion with harshness and using individual personalities as inspiration. She earned her degree in fashion design from Beckmans College of Design in Stockholm.

1. UNTITLED, 2009 • Personal 2. OWN, 2009 • Personal
3. OWN, 2009 • Personal 4. WINTER MAIN 2010 •
Editorial – No.1–5, OWN, 2009, Personal

Courtney Brims

Courtney Brims is a Brisbane based artist who graduated with a degree in interior design before turning her
attention to illustration in 2008. Her drawings are influenced by Victoriana, ghost stories, old photographs,
daydreams, and nightmares. Working with pencils, Brims creates dreamy worlds of lost girls and bewildering
creatures, focusing on the beauty of nature and its domination over time. She has had solo shows at
LA's Black Maria Gallery and most recently at Brisbane's Nine Lives Gallery, as well as numerous group
shows across Australia.

masa
ki
mizu
no

SECRET HOUSE 2010, Personal 2, MODELING BEACH 2010,
Personal 3, THINKING GIRL, 2009, Personal 4, HIGH SCHOOL GIRL,
2010, Personal 5, FLOWER 2010, Personal

Japanese artist Masaki Mizuno graduated from Bunka Fashion College with a degree in men's design.
Since then she has kept herself busy with several exhibitions in Tokyo, lectures at Parsons, Vantan Design
Institute, and her alma mater. She has contributed illustrations to Clear magazine, View2 Publications,
and Fashion Color magazine.

martine
johanna

From childhood on, drawing had been an escape for Martine Johanna. In 2006, after ten
years working as a women's fashion designer, she decided to make a career out of it.
Today, the Dutch illustrator still retains an affinity for fashion in its extreme and cultural forms,
but blends this with artisan crafts. Johanna's work reveals part of her personality,
a slightly darker side with an undertow of sexual tension.

1. YELLOW, 2010. Personal 2. HER, 2010. Personal
3. FOXICRAFTS, 2010. Personal – All IN by Kim & Bach
2010. Personal 5. THE WOLVES, 2010. Personal

hanna müller

1. FRAUD, 2009. Personal 2. SHOW OFF, 2009. Personal
3. SITTE, 2009. Personal 4. GWENCH!, 2010. Personal
5. TRANSPARENT, 2009. Personal 6. ESTEFANI, 2009. Personal
7. JUST LIKE US, 2009. Personal

For as long as she can remember, drawing and painting have been Hanna Müller's biggest interests. Born in 1989, the Swedish artist used to draw as a means of relaxation and personal gratification – before realizing that she could make a living out of it. Since this epiphany, she works part-time as an illustrator.

fernanda guedes

Brazilian artist Fernanda Guedes has done several magazines and book covers, advertisement campaigns, and editorial illustrations for clients such as Vogue, Veja, Marie Claire, Panda Books, Objetiva, J.W.Thompson, Africa, Ogilvy, Leo Burnett, and DM9DDB. She has exhibited extensively in São Paulo and in 2008 was nominated for the Press Shortlist at Cannes Festival for her work with Leo Burnett and Coral.

1. FRIENDS IN FEATHERS, 2009. Personal 2. MAKE UP YOUR EYES, 2009. Personal 3. FEATHER HEAD BAND, 2009. Personal 4. BLACK HAT, 2009. Personal 5. PINK NAILS, 2008. Personal

pomme chan

1. THE AGE OF FEMININE, 2009. Exhibition –
Personal 2. LADY AND HER BAGS, 2010.
Exhibition – Personal 3. LUST FOR SHOE,
2009. Exhibition – Personal 4. LUST FOR
LOVE, 2009. Exhibition – Personal 5. LARA,
2010. Exhibition – Personal

Born and educated in Bangkok, Pomme Chan completed her bachelor of interior design at Silpakorn University before working at the Bangkok offices of both WPP's DY&R and Grey as a graphic designer. In 2002 she relocated to the U.K. for a foundation in graphic design and communication at the London College of Communication. Her drawings have been featured in the Telegraph, idN, Grafik, and Curvy Book, and she has worked on prestigious ad campaigns for the likes of Sony, MTV, Volkswagen, Mercedes-Benz, Marc Jacobs, Microsoft, the Guardian, Nike, and Topshop. Using her unique hand-drawn skill, Pomme's eclectic style gets its inspiration from everyday life. Nature, fashion, architecture, and the female form play a big part in her work.

makiko sugawa

Call them dark or downright strange, but there's no denying that Makiko Sugawa's illustrations are electrified with eroticism. Women are clad in lacy lingerie and posed suggestively with a bevy of sexual accessories. But look a little deeper and you'll notice that many possess prosthetic limbs or no legs at all. Such a unique vision and commentary on women, beauty, and fashion – the artificiality of it, the mechanics of it – have earned the Japanese artist her own solo exhibition at Space Yui Tokyo and a picture book, Ni and Meme, published in 2009. Sugawa graduated from the Kyoto University of Art and Design, and belongs to the design office Kokokumaru Co., ltd.

1 BASKET, 2009. Exhibition – Space Yui Gallery. 2. CAT WOMEN, 2007.
Exhibition – Space Yui Gallery. 3. PARROT, 2007. Kokokumaru Co., ltd.
4. LACE QUEEN, 2007. Kokokumaru Co., ltd. 5. LACE CAMISOLE,
2009. Exhibition – Space Yui Gallery.

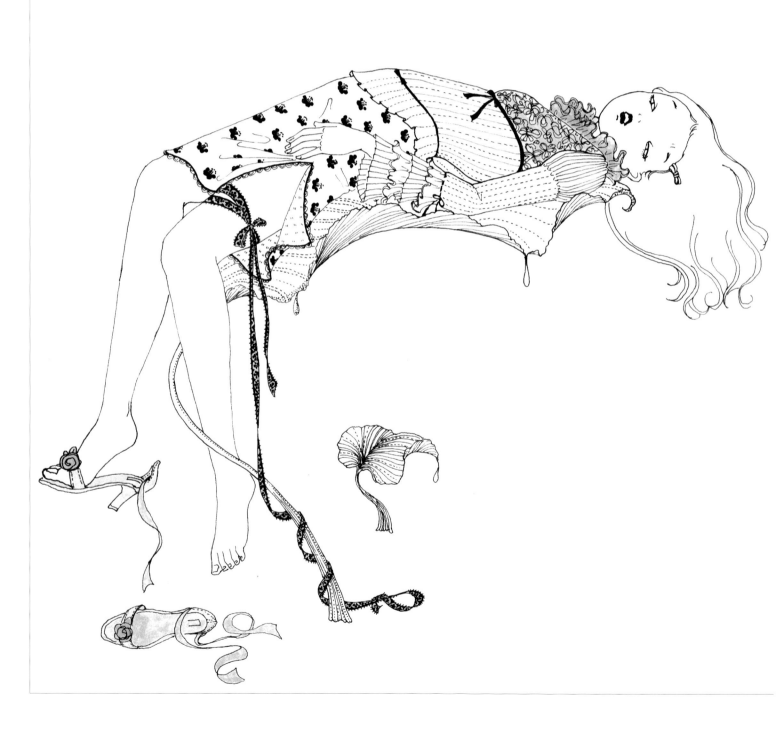

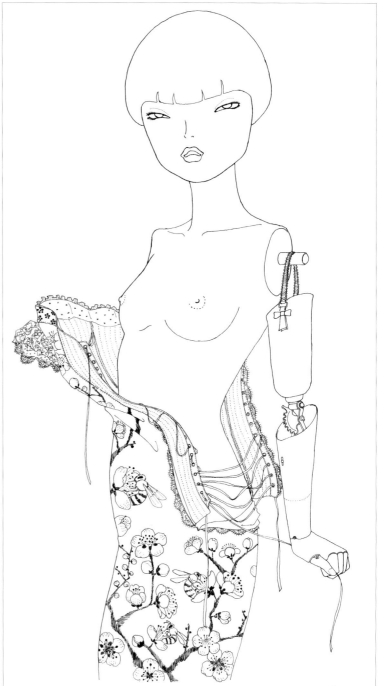

1. EVIL, 2007, Compound Gallery. 2. MACHINETTE, 2009, Exhibition – Space for design. 3. DRESS UP, PLAY, 2009, Exhibition – Space for design. 4. RABBIT, 2008, Exhibition – Space for design. 5. SMOKE, 2007 – www.amandavisell.com

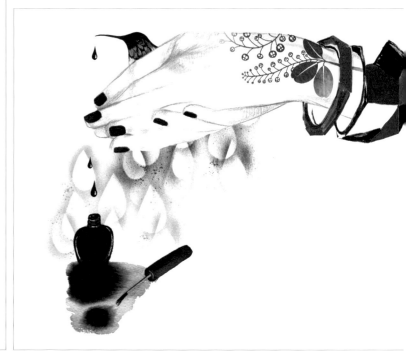

mia over gaar d

English 2004 Beyond 3 —Mungo-Push 2006 Concept 3 no-Willd-2007 Present Gear 4 TORTURE 2006 Advertising Pictures/80s The Door Show ■ WOMAN April 2007 Present

A graduate of Denmark's Designskole, Mia Overgaard has studied art, illustration and fashion design. Since graduation, her work has revolved mostly around commercial and fashion illustration. She creates realistic yet surreal and detailed illustrations of people and animals living in a dream-like universe — happy, beautiful creatures, yet at times depicted with a shadow of melancholy across their faces. Clients include Marie Claire, SELF, Glamour, Neiman Marcus, RSCG, Taschen, Volkswagen, and Gap.

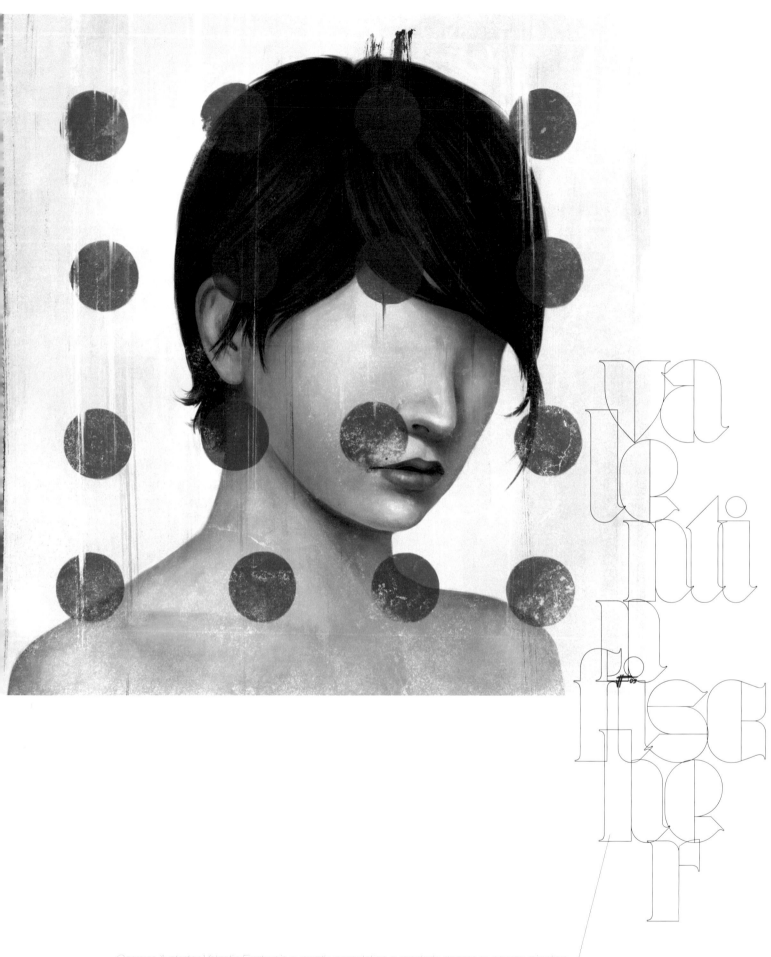

German illustrator Valentin Fischer is currently completing a master's degree in communication, planning, and design at the HfG Schwäbisch Gmünd. His work often moody and melancholy paintings with elements reminiscent of childhood (such as toys and balloons), has earned him international attention.

1. LA CASA LIBRE, 2009. *Personal.* 2. DANS L'HIVER FROID, 2009. *Personal.* 3. IN A OF PAST DAYS, 2010. *Personal.* 4. CARNIVAL DESIRES, 2008. *Personal.* 5. DEAD BALLOON, 2007. *Personal.*

gildo medina

1. ENVY, 2013, Amsterdam – *In Mix*
2/3. FASHION VICTIMS II, 2010 *Editorial*
Vanity Teen, en. 4. HEROES DAYS IN MONO UNIVERSE
2010. *Persona* – Galerie 12 Jeanette Mariani, Paris
5. FASHION VICTIMS II, 2010, *Retour – Palais Liberation*

*Paris, London, Mexico, New York, Tokyo, Berlin – there is no denying Gildo Medina's international appetite.
Having worked in six different countries and with 25 prizes and awards already under his belt, the visual artist
and photographer creates illustrations that smack of a cosmopolitan sophistication. He typically
transplants drawings made from classical pencils and brushes into a digital atmosphere, producing
images that vary in gesture, fashion, and attitude – but all with the primary focus on beauty.*

19

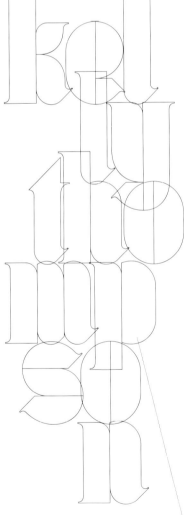

kelly thompson

1. HALINA, 2009 (Nations – *The Island Heart*) 2. NIGHT EYES, 2009 (Nations – *Childhood*) 3. ONE, (2009) 4. LITTLE DOVE, 2009 (Nations – *Ruby Redruth*) 5. SUITHE, 2008 (Nations – *A.D.*), 2008 (Gallery Print – *People commission*)

Freelance photographer and illustrator Kelly Thompson graduated from Massey University in 2004 with a bachelor's degree in design. Since then she has exhibited internationally and has a wide range of commercial clients, including banks, to fashion brands, and skin care companies. She describes her work as "refined yet sensual and suggestive." Her prints have proven to be very popular and are now selling worldwide.

gabriel moreno

Based in Madrid, Gabriel Moreno has been working in different design studios and ad agencies in Andalusia since graduating from the University of Sevilla in fine arts. Beyond his illustration work for wide-ranging agencies, brands, and publications, he engraves and paints for personal fulfilment. He likens the two as coming from the same motivations – the sensuality through graphics and the elegance of the black outline.

1. MARLBORO 2008 Advertising – Marlboro Agency La Despensa
2. FUJIBO 2008 Fabore 3. KEELA 2010 Fabore 4. BC 2010
Advertising – Stuf 5. CHINA 2010 Fabore 6. GUSTAVO DUDAMEL
2009 Fabore – Los Angeles Times Magazine

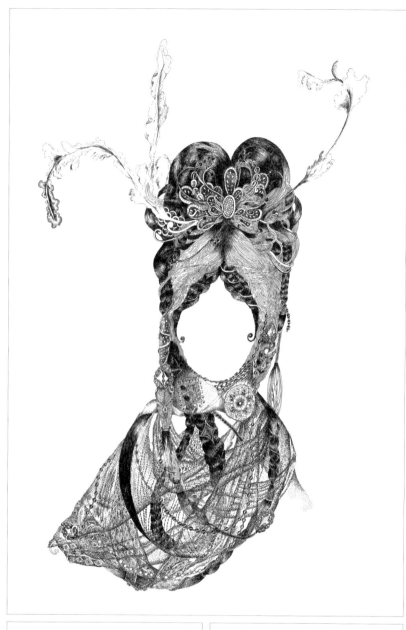

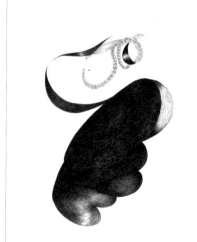

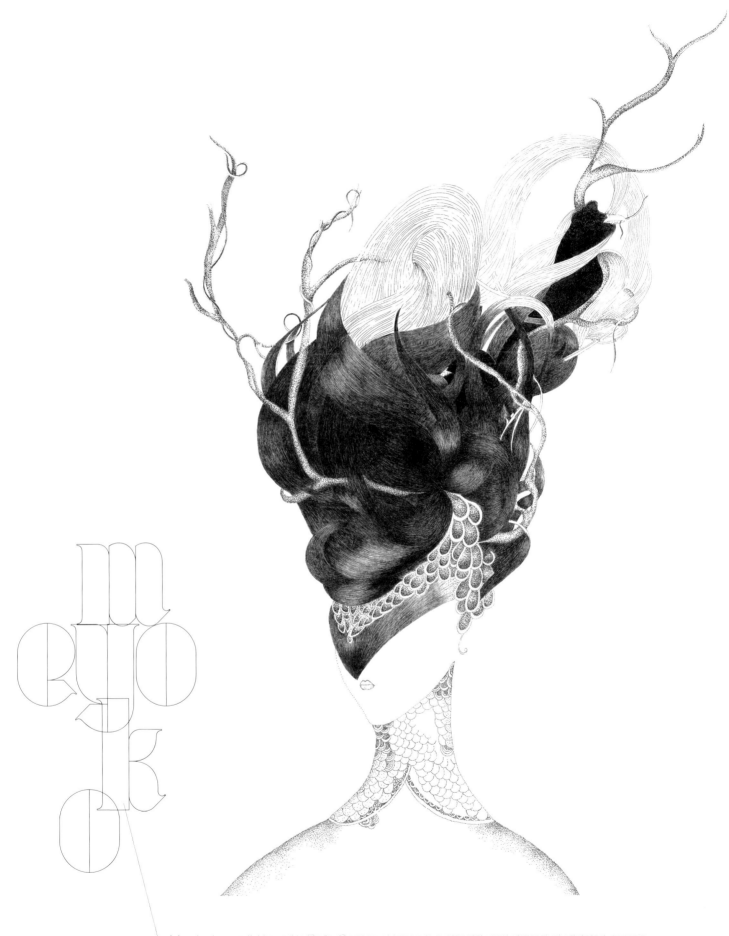

MEYOKO

Meyoko is an artist based in Berlin, Germany. Her work is intricately and obsessively detailed, organic, and intense. She likens the process of drawing to "singing from the depths of the soul" and is greatly influenced by her time spent in the Amazon. As such, plants, insects, birds, and living organisms emerge out of her dreamy lines and swirls, leading one down strange and hallucinatory pathways. Meyoko's works have been exhibited internationally and published in fashion and lifestyle magazines in Paris, London, New York, Barcelona, and more.

1 Violin, 2010. Pencil, 2.5HL, 2010. Pencil
2 Black. 1.2. Pen. Pencil 3. R. 20 x N. Pencil
3 OR HIRADA. 2010. Pencil 6. HJERU
2010. Pencil

jennymörtsell

Jenny Mörtsell is an illustrator from Stockholm, Sweden. She graduated from Konstfack University of Arts in crafts and design in 2004. Since then she has been working full time, creating illustrations for magazines, advertising, books, and fashion. She is currently based in New York.

1. HUMAN BEHAVIOUR, 2010. Editorial – Line A Journal 2. VESTOJ, 2010. Editorial – Vestoj 3. BLANK BOOKS, 2010. Editorial – Present 4. JULIA H..., 2009. Personal 5. LINDGA-W., 2009. Personal 6. STRIPES, 2009. Personal

sarah arman

Fashion illustrator Sarah Harman focuses on the structure and expression of the face, as well as the movement and texture of hair. Her distinctive style uses bold and energetic marks that enliven her work. She aims to enhance cosmetic products in a thoroughly new and refreshing way within the editorial context.

hannaviktorsson

Hanna Viktorsson was born in Sweden in 1987 and studied graphic design at the University of Cumbria, England. Shortly after graduation in 2009, she returned to Sweden, where she is based now. Her illustrations are mainly focused on people, expressions, and fashion. She likes to keep it simple, often excluding both the background and parts of the person portrayed. She does most of her work by hand with a simple pen and pencil on cheap paper.

1 / 2 / 4 / 5 / 6 UNTITLED 2010 Personal
3 UNTITLED 2010 Handsome Lifestyle

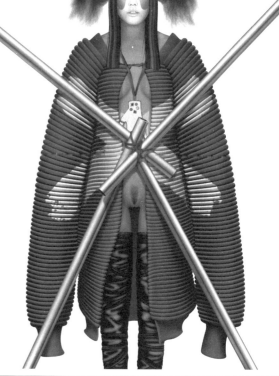

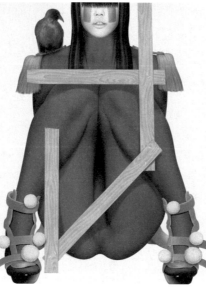
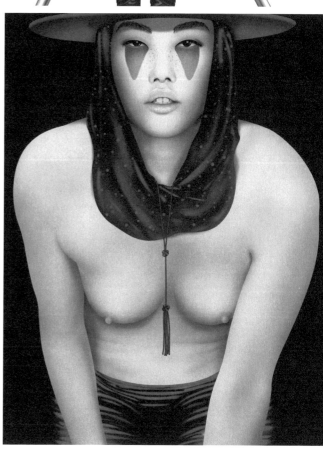

jesse auersalo

Visual artist Jesse Auersalo has drummed up a lot of interest in his native Finland, London, and New
York, where he current lives and works. Chalk it up to his startlingly unique brand of work: dark,
character-driven illustrations that illicit strong reactions from the viewer. He currently divides his time
between Brooklyn and Helsinki and is represented by Pekka Finland and Big Active in London.

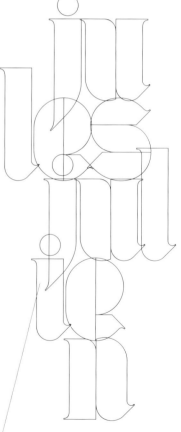

Born in 1975, Paris-based artist and illustrator Jules Julien constantly questions the drift and the shift of the world that surrounds us. In conceptual terms, he puts forth a scene in a world where symbols blend with stories, and the strange is concealed behind the images in his meticulously produced drawings. He has been featured in galleries in Europe, the United States, and Australia and the Diesel Denim Gallery in Tokyo printed t-shirts with his design. He is represented by Valérie Oualid in Europe and Mitani Woo in Asia.

1/2/5 RÉBUS, 2009 Collective show – Nuit Blanche – La Chapelle des Calvairiennes, centre d'art Mayenne/France 3/4 RELEASE, 2009 Editorial – Untitled Magazine – Curated by Hugo&Marie, US 6 BRUCE, 2009 Collective show No Man's Land – French Embassy – Tokyo/Japan

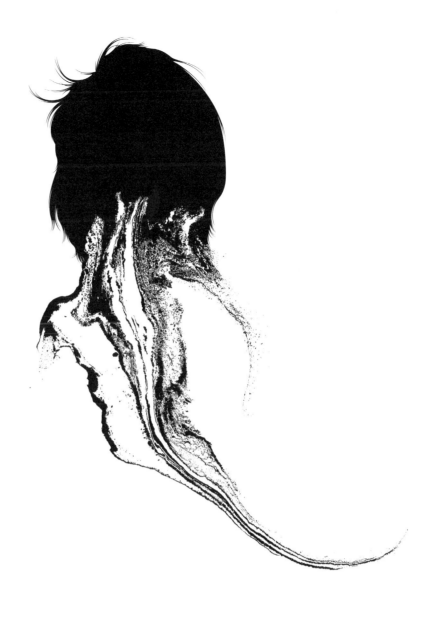

hiroshi tanabe

Hiroshi Tanabe's vibrant illustrations mirror the graphic line work of traditional Japanese woodcuts. His illustrations have evolved into more refined and layered drawings throughout his career, marrying old world beauty and modernity in a way that is thoroughly fresh. In 1994, he won British Vogue's esteemed Vogue/Sotheby's Cecil Beaton Award for fashion illustration. In 1997, Pucci International commissioned him to design a collection of mannequins and wall graphics. His range of clients include Anna Sui, Shiseido, the New York Times, The New Yorker, Rolling Stone, British Vogue, Le Sportsac, GAP, Barneys New York, Ann Taylor, and Sony. Born in Kanagawa, Japan, Hiroshi Tanabe graduated from Tama Art College and Accademia di Brera in Milan.

1. SAYOKO YAMAGUCHI #2, 2008. Editorial – Achtung. 2. FEI KAWAKUBO, 2008. Editorial – Wallpaper. 3. SAYOKO YAMAGUCHI #1, 2008. Editorial – Achtung. 4. COMME DES GARÇONS, 2001. Editorial – NOVA. 5. FROM COLLECTION #3, 2004. Editorial – SlNagazine. 6. UNTITLED, 2001. Web-site – Bumble and bumble. 7. UNTITLED, 2008. Editorial – Nico.

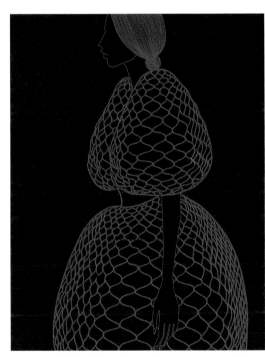

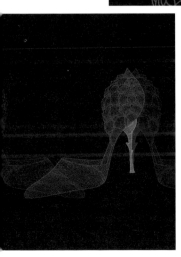

i
ra
na
do
u
er

Born in 1984, Argentine artist Irana Douer has already commanded a formidable following with
her highly sensitive portraits of women in deep thought and sometimes curious positions.
Her illustrations, mostly crafted on thick paper with acrylic paint, utilize hirsute associations to
powerful effect by using hair as a medium to express power, sex, and beauty. She is
currently an art student in Buenos Aires and the curator of a monthly online magazine Ruby Mag

Miss Blackbirdy

Miss Blackbirdy, née Merel Boers, graduated from the Gerrit Rietveld Academy in Amsterdam in 2006. With numerous awards under her belt, including the Lancôme Colour Designs Award, BLVD Fashion Award and the Piep Westendorp Stimulation Prize, the artist has been recognized for her distinct talent, which she categorizes as "story-sewing." The story-sewing technique involves using thread to make illustrations into three-dimensional drawings on paper, clothing, or jewelry. Miss Blackbirdy has illustrated for clients like Elle Girl, CosmoGirl, The Dutch Ministry of Culture & Science, Port of Amsterdam, War Child, Levis, and Success Stationery.

1 TEXTILE PRINT, 2008. Personal 2. ELLY AND THE FLOWERS TEXTILE PRINT, 2008. Studio Miss Blackbird. 3. ELLY AND THE FLOWERS, 2008. Editorial – Studio Miss Blackbird. Character and print design for fashion show. 5. CITY KEY, 2010. Editorial – Success – Organizing systems stationery.

YUKO FURUSHO

willbroome

Artist Will Broome's work process is self-described as "naive," but behind the happy-go-lucky facade lurks something a bit darker. Broom's drawings can sometimes be found on walls and in books, although mostly they are used on clothing. He enjoys working with fashion designers such as Marc Jacobs, Gucci, Missoni, and Wedgowood.

1. PURPLE PANDA, 2009. Private commission 2. GREEN PANDA, 2009. Personal 3. YELLOW OWL, 2008. Personal 4. BEARS, 2007. Personal 5. RED PANDA, 2007. Personal

1 UNTITLED 2010 Peroxy 2 POSH ONES 2007 Peroxy
3 UNTITLED, 2010 Peroxy 4 BEAR, 2007 Chalk animation
5 OWL AND BEAR, 2007 Peroxy 6 OINK, 2007 Chalk animation
7 WILLEM DAFOE, 2007 Peroxy

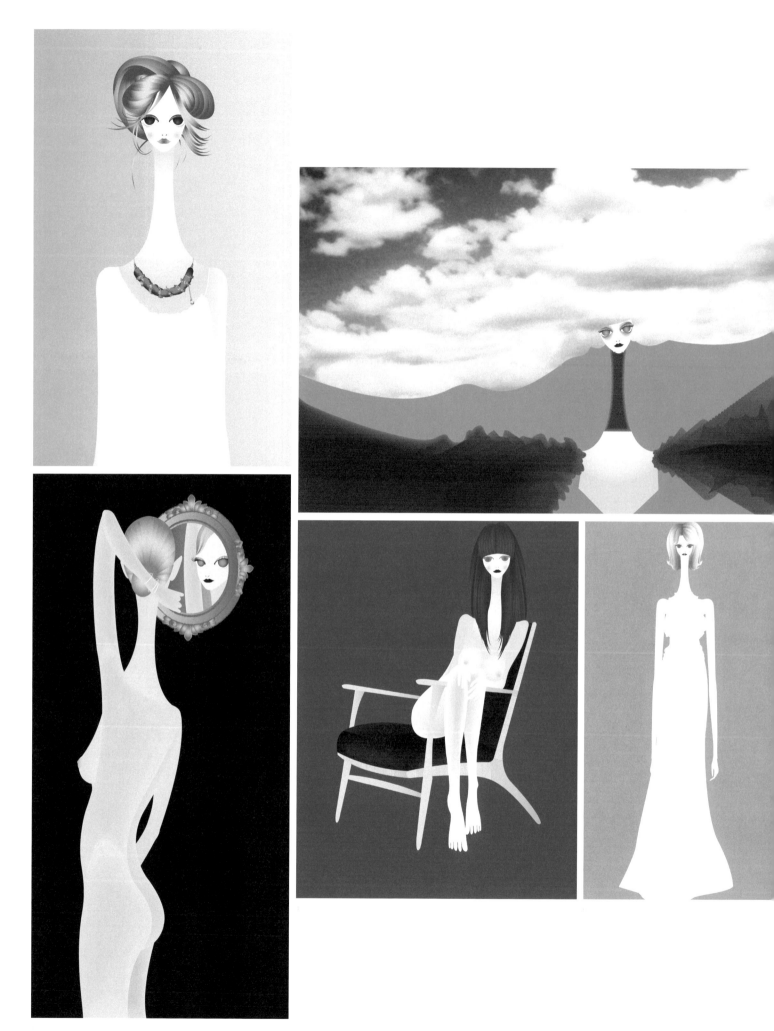

ed
ts
u
wa
ki

1. BLANCHE, 2002 *Editorial - Vogue Gioiello*. 2. TRUTH, 2003 *Editorial -* VITAMER, 2003 *Editorial -* 3. AVAN, 2003 *Editorial - Maison Rouge* 5. BLANDIE, 2004 *Editorial – Vogue Gioiello* 6. LATE SUMMER

Artist and illustrator Ed TSUWAKI was born in Hiroshima, Japan in 1966 and has done countless female portraits for fashion magazines and advertisements.

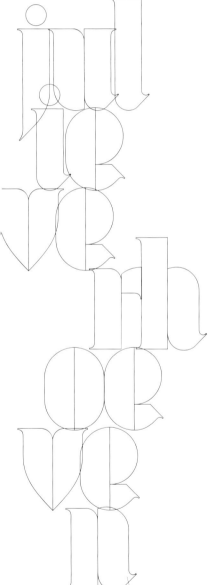

Tour de force Julie Verhoeven has collaborated with fashion powerhouses such as Versace, Topshop, Louis Vuitton, and Mulberry, bands such as Primal Scream and Fischerpooner, and has shown at the toniest galleries across England. Chalk it up to the London-based, multidisciplinary artist's formidable years of 'experience': she has an eye for surrealism and Schiele, the result of which are illustrations of bold, fearless women, who both exemplify the raw and the real ethos of femininity. She has published two books, Pat Bottomed Girls, and Gas Book.

1. HIT ME WITH A FLOWER, 2010, *Invitation – Marella*
2. CHOP + PLATO, 2008, *Sky HO HO – Sky HO*
3. MEDUSA, 2008, *Textile print design (detail) – Versace*
4. JOLIE SHOPPER, 2007, *Bag – Mulberry*, 5. HO HO HO,
2008, *Christmas Card – The Royal College of Art*

1. QUEER AS A CATS FART 2006, Dessin/Installation —
Acryl,Leinw. 2 ... TE UP YOUR FART AND FLY 2007,
Installation — Objekt, Holz, Verschiedene 3. JOEY + DAVID
2004 ... Skulptur/Installation — Acryl, Leinwand 4. BLOW 2006,
Objekt/Installation — H&M 5. BLUE MOOD 2010,
Objekt/Installation — Kohle 6. VERY HEAVY VILLAGE
2006, Exhibition/Installation — Rittersalon

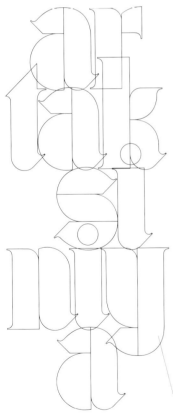

1. CHARER PEARL POWDER, 2010. Personal 2. DICE FANCY SHOES, 2010. Personal 3. MIU MIU DRESS, 2010. Personal 4. PERFUME ADDICT, 2010. Personal 5. VICTOR & ROLF DRESS, 2010. Personal 6. ERICKSON BEAMON JEWELS, 2010. Personal.

Russian-born artist Missyutah Kseniya, aka Artaksniya, is inspired by fashion, literature, and traveling, the impressions from which she tries to convey in her pictures. Her aim is to serve beauty by doing her personal best, whether it be through her fashion illustrations, graphic design work, or textile designs.

autu
nnn
whi
teh
urst

1. SUGAR & SKIN, 2007, Editorial – London Telegraph.
2. CHLOE PURCE, 2005, Editorial – London Telegraph. 3. COLOR,
2009, Editorial – Computer Arts. 4. WINTER, 2006, editorial – London
Telegraph. 5. WISH YOU WERE HERE, 2004,
self-promotion, Art Department.

Born in New Orleans, now working out of Brooklyn, New York, Autumn Whitehurst
made a permanent commitment to fashion at art school in Baltimore. Her sleek photo-realistic
illustrations have made her unique in the illustration industry and have landed her
editorial, advertising, and CD cover work for such clients as Penguin Books, British and
American Elle, Ogilvy and Mathers, American Eagle Outfitters, and more.

5 VOLTES, 2007, Self-promotion – Art Department
1 FALL, 2004, Editorial – March Hare 3 TAYLOR+, 2005, Editorial –
London Telegraph 4 INTEREST, 2006, Editorial – London Telegraph
5 CHRISTINA AGUILERA, 2007, Editorial – Blender 6 VALUETERS, 2007,
Editorial – Jalouse 7 Lily, 2006, 2006, Self-promotion – Art Department
8 FLORA+FAUNA, 2007, Self-promotion – Art Department

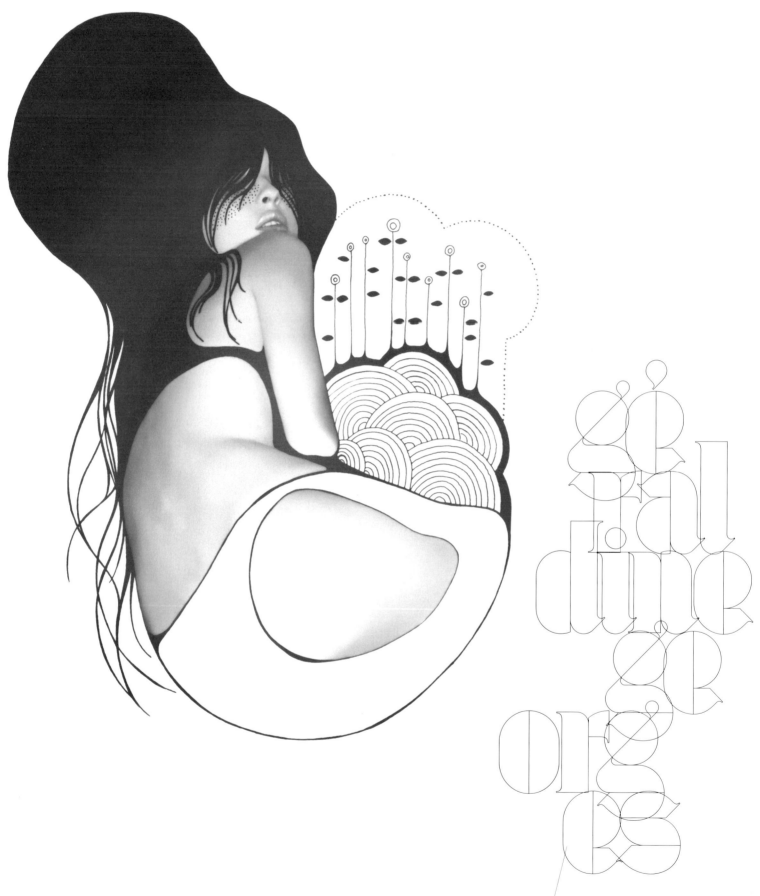

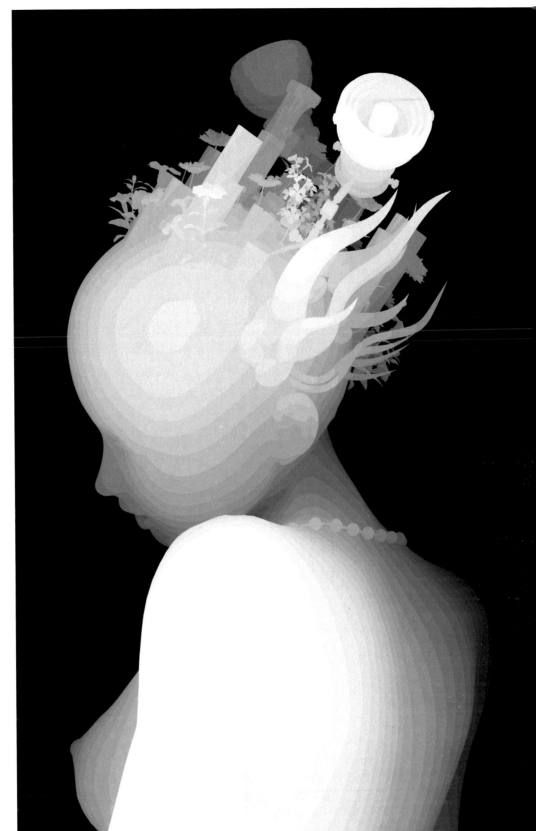

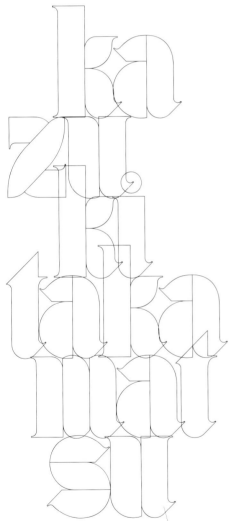

kazuki takamatsu

1 I WANT TO GO SOMEWHERE, 2009, *Painting* 2 WITH ME, 2009, *Painting* 3 THE BEST BOUQUET IN THIS WEEK, 2009, *Painting* 4 SEASONING, 2009, *Painting* 5 DESIRE, 2009, *Painting*

Artist Kazuki Takamatsu creates astonishing paintings, which show off a real command of technique. His dark, ethereal, icy black-and-white illustrations of women, guns, chaos, and other suggestive scenarios betray two unique techniques. First is his use of gouache – he can take a three-dimensional sculpture or object and commit it to paper. Second, he has mastered what he calls "depth map", in which an impossible palette of gray is utilized to color every pixel in its exact, proportionally distant shade. He was born in 1978 and graduated from the Tohoku University of Art and Design.

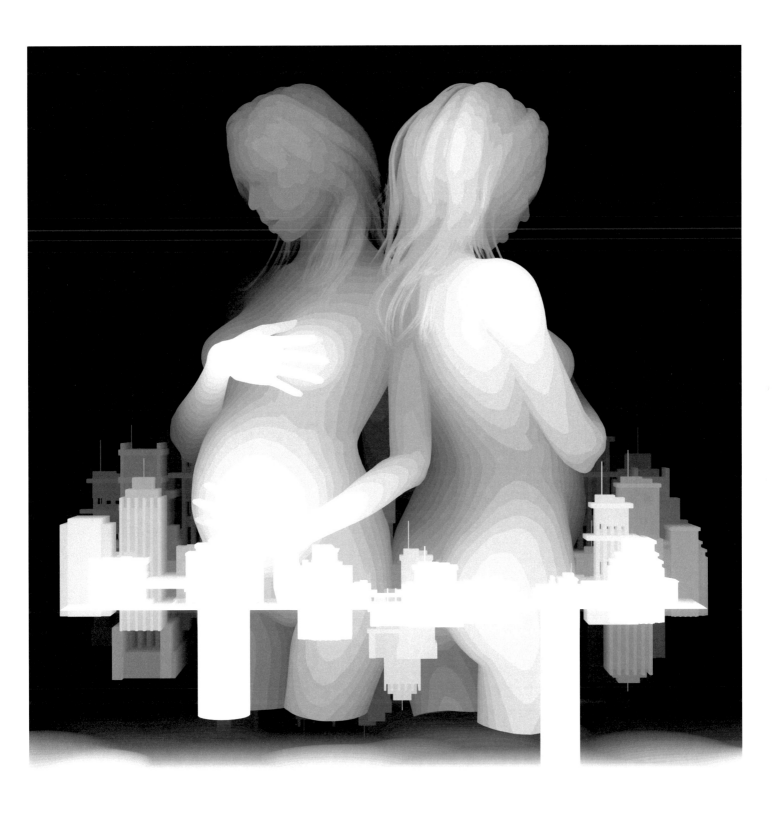

COMMISSIONED BY THE 14A EXCLUSIVELY FOR PRINTS LIVE
PEN-PAPER-SCISSORS · 26 JUNE 2009

JOE McLAREN (DUTCH UNCLE) and
YEHRIN TONG (DEBUT ART)

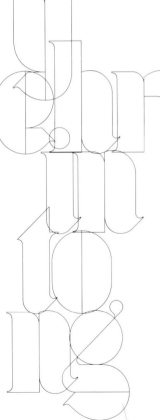

1. *Yuki*, 2010. *Pesani* 2, FAUGR., 2010. *Pesani* MERVAD., 2010. *Pesani* 4, VA, 2010. *Pesani* 5. !BSHI, 2010. *Pesani*

The words "minimal" and "simple" rarely come in artist Yehrin Tong's vocabulary. Her main interests lie in creating illusory, eye-boggling, yet mathematically-inspired typographic illustrations. These can be seen for ad campaigns on billboards and taxi cabs, embroidery prints for fashion brands, typographic covers, and editorials. Tong graduated from Central Saint Martins with a BA in graphic design, and has worked with independent music artists who she met while regularly haunting the underground club scene in London.

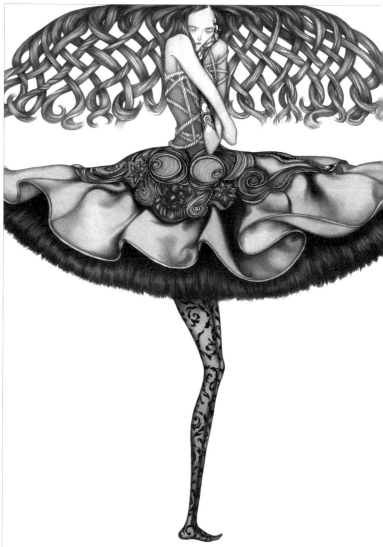

laura laine

1. REFUGEE, 2004, Betori - Florence
2. EXPLOSION, 2004, Painting - Red Feather
3. NIPPITTA, 2004, Exhibition - Design Week Helsinki
Neuhardfalls #103, TA, 2003
Editorial - Wallpaper, Finland

Although she studied fashion design at the University of Art and Design Helsinki, Laura Laine always focused on fashion illustration; coming into her own as a freelance fashion illustrator was only natural. Her work can be characterized as a little dark, deeply stylized, with a certain flair for action and the avant-garde. Her recent clients include a who's who list in the fashion world, including Zara, Rad Hourani, the New York Times, T Magazine, Tommy Hilfiger, ElleGirl, the Guardian, H&M, and Daniel Palillo. She currently lives in Helsinki, Finland.

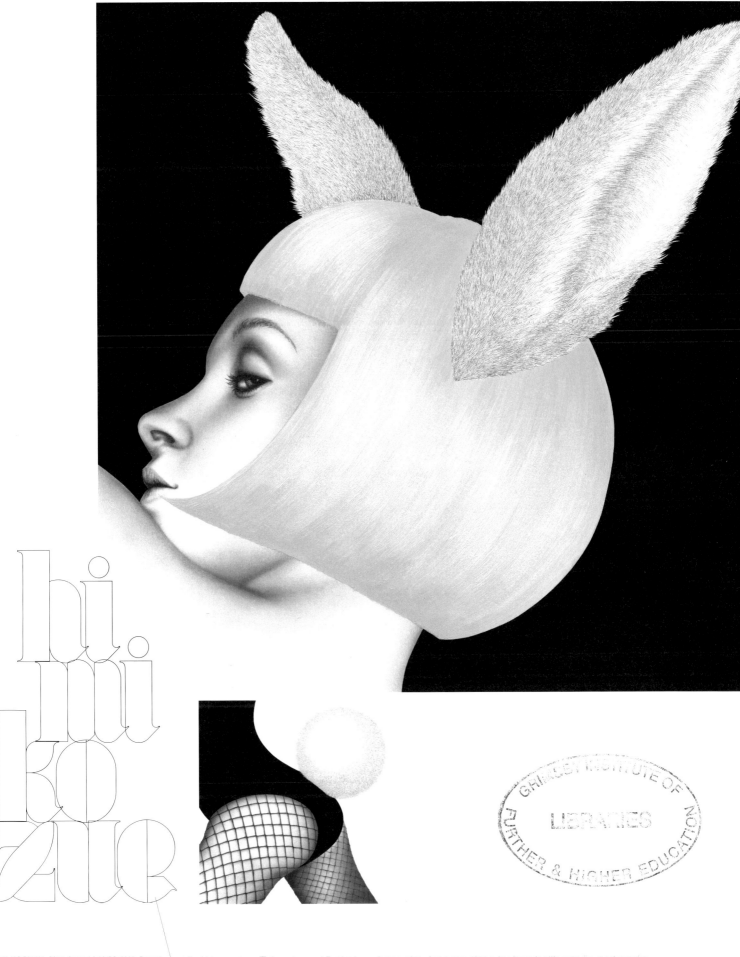

hi.
mi.
ko
zue

1. CAT AND RABBIT, 2010, Fanzine 2. MUSE, 2010, Fanzine
3. DRAGONFLY AND HAT, 2010, Fanzine 4. RABBIT AND MINES,
2010, Fanzine 5. FLIRT DRESS, 2010, Fanzine
6. FUTON GIRL, 2010, Fanzine 7. BUNNY GIRL, 2010, Fanzine

Himi Kozue is a Tokyo-based illustrator whose drawings are done by hand with acrylic, watercolor,
charcoal, pastel, pen, and pencil. She works with a variety of media and genres.
Her illustrations have been included in publications such as the New York Times Magazine.

lina
bo
dén

1. UNTITLED, 2008, *Personal – Drawing from an original photo by photographer Rauan Dessanov.* 2. UNTITLED, 2008, *Personal – Drawing from an original photo by photographer Rauan Dessanov.* 3. THE GLOBAL, 2009, 2010, *Exhibition – Exhibited and featuring PASS in Stockholm.* 4. SPREAD TO RICHES!, 2009, *Privat, MONE Fashion Magazine.* 5. THE GLOBAL, 2009, 2010, *Freelance – Freelance Freelancing, PASS in Stockholm.*

Born in Stockholm in 1980, freelance illustrator Lina Bodén has worked at H&M as
a print assistant and for the Swedish fashion brand Monki. Prior to graduating
from the Beckmans College of Design in graphic design in 2008, she studied painting
at Konstskolan Idun Lovén and Gerlesborgsskolan.

Lina Ekstrand

Since 2003, Lina Ekstrand has been working as a freelance illustrator in Scandinavia and
the broader Europe region. She works artistically and conceptually with strategic
communication, focusing on strong visual language to communicate her ideas. She graduated
with a bachelor's degree in visual communication at Denmark's Design School. She also
holds degrees in illustration and graphic design from the London College of Communication.
She has exhibited her work in London, Mexico, and Sweden.

FASHION TALE, 2008. Editorial - Fashion Tale
magazine 2 /5. PERSONAL, 2010. Editorial -
Personal 3/4. COSTUME MAGAZINE, 2010.
Editorial - Costume.

Sabine Pieper

Berlin-based artist and photographer Sabine Pieper whips up soft, feminine drawings that explore the narrative between romance, beauty, and the self. Her work often features faces repeating, as if in a mirror, suggesting the idea of consciousness and self-image.

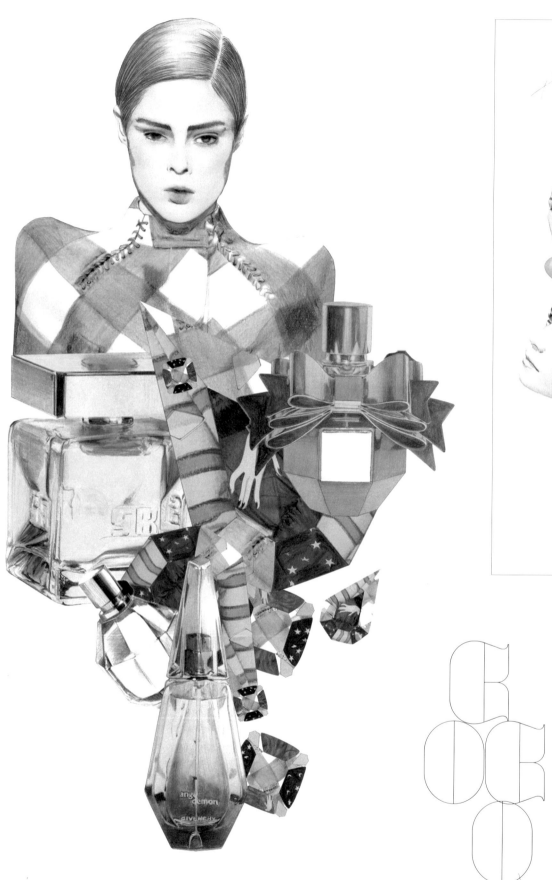

French designer and graphic artist Coco honed her craft studying fine arts in Paris before moving to London in 2004, where she set up creative and technology consultancy getconfused.net. She is interested in subliming dream-like scenarios with bold graphic compositions, which can be seen in her lifestyle accessories of turban head pieces and cushions sold at Barneys, Colette, and Harvey Nichols. Coco typically experiments with traditional processes such as painting, drawing, and ceramics before designing the final digital image. She now divides her time between commissioned illustration work and trend reports for diverse fashion magazines including Elle, Vogue, Nylon, and Muse.

1. PERFUME MONTAGE, 2009. Editorial – Plastique Magazine
2. 080 BARCELONA FASHION WEEK, 2008. Exhibition –
080 Barcelona Fashion Week 3. ASOS SPECIAL SCARF 2009.
Collection Forget Me Not – asos.com 4. MECHANISM 2, 2010.
Exhibition – Gallery Nucleus 5. NYLON US, 2008. Editorial – Nylon USA
6 + 7. FORGET ME NOT COLLECTION, 2009. Collection Forget Me Not

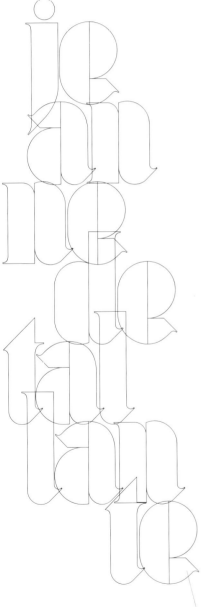

jeanne detallante

*French artist Jeanne Detallante lives and works in New York. Her dramatic
illustrations for the likes of Italian Vogue, Marie Claire Belgium, and Sony Music Japan,
toy with themes of identity and of a more glamorous yesteryear by applying
a clear love for costume and color. In collaboration with Repetto & Petit, Detallante
recently produced a line of silk scarves for Carven at Colette in Paris.*

MIU MIU

SONIA RYKIEL

wendy plovmand

From in Denmark, based in London, Wendy Plovmand has been working as a professional artist and illustrator since she graduated from the Design School of Denmark in 2001. Though she has dabbled in fashion design, graphic design, and art direction, she now focuses purely on art and illustration. Plovmand's style sublimes poetic feminine elements with edgy fashion and a fairy tale sense of the super natural. Clients include Topshop, Cosmo Girl, Flare magazine, the Guardian, Johnson & Johnson, Unicef, The Royal Theater of Denmark, and The Republic of Fritz Hansen.

1. WEALTH WALLS, 2009, Wallpaper, Wal--in-teriors, Hamburg
2. ELLE GIRL COVER, 2009, Cover illustration—Elle Girl, Korea
3. MUST-HAVE LEGGINGS, 2009, Editorial—Eurowoman, EGMONT
4. MUST-HAVE TROUSERS, 2009, Editorial, Eurowoman, EGMONT
5. SHOPPING, 2009, Editorial, Eurowoman, EGMONT

71

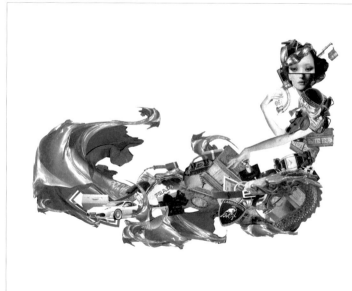

maren esdar

Maren Esdar was born in 1972 in Germany. Educated as a stylist and illustrator in Hamburg and London, she finds that her illustrations inspire her design and vice versa. Her extravagantly surreal and stylized collages — composed both by hand and computer — have been published in the world's most influential fashion and style magazines. Her work has been featured in numerous books, such as Illusive 2, All Allure, A Book Designed to Help, and Wonderland

1. ELEMICA, 2010, Advertising pitch – Jergens Naturals for GAGE UK
1/2/3. RICH IVA, EUROPA, COSMETICS, 2008, Editorial – Hauts Nine magazine
4. SOLD UITGEVERIJ TO CHINA, 2008, Editorial – OG, No. 6 – LUCHERA
10. + Exhibition Maren Esdar 2010 in Berlin – Personal & ARACHNOPHOBIA,
2010 – Exhibition Maren Esdar 2010 in Berlin – Personal

Paris-based illustrator and artist Alexandra Compain-Tissier's extensive oeuvre of work encompasses watercolor paintings and illustrations for the likes of Martin Margiela, Zet Magazine, and Saks Fifth Avenue. Her work often takes a celebrity bent for fashion-based publications, including the New York Times, Conde Nast Travelor, Glamour, and Nylon. She is represented by the American advertising agency Art Department.

alexandra compain-tissier

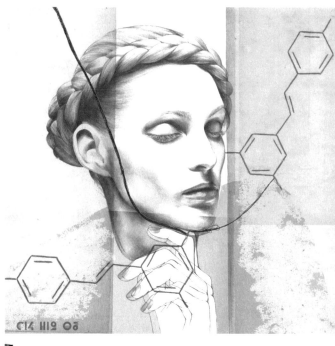

KLAARTJE EN KEETJE.

ATELIER UNIVERSAL
Carl Klein.

HELSINKI

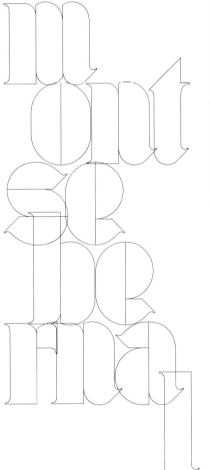
montse bernal

1. ELENA, 2008. *Editorial – 'One hundred portraits, two birds and one love song' project.* 2. BEAUTY THE NEXT GENERATION, 2008. *Editorial – Magazine La Vanguardia.* 3. UNTITLED, 2009/2010. *Art Gallery – 'Embroidering & Whispering' Project.* 5. CORDELIA, 2008. *Editorial – 'One hundred portraits, two birds and one love song' project.* 6. THE VEIL, 2008. *Editorial – Magazine La Vanguardia.*

Barcelona based illustrator Montse Bernal sharpened her illustration skills at the École Nationale Superieure des Arts Décoratifs in Paris and at the University of Barcelona. She was born in 1976.

RUSS MILLS

With nearly 20 years of crafting skills experience, freelance illustrator Russ Mills now pursues the traditional gallery and exhibition path. His current work is a clash of styles from classical to pop surrealism, focusing predominantly on the human form by abstracting elements from nature and the animal kingdom. He covers subjects such as superficiality and isolation progressing into more socio-political expressions. He graduated with a degree in experimental film and animation from Leeds Metropolitan University in 1995.

1. LUCI_FOUR, 2009. Limited edition 2. HOYA CARNOSA, 2008. Limited edition 3. ASPHYXIA, 2010. Limited edition 4. AEONIUM, 2008. Limited edition 5. FANTASTAPLEX, 2007. Limited edition.

hachimitsu
mama

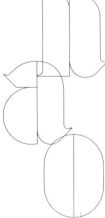

Artist Nao's work has been included in numerous shows and publications around the globe, including Nylon
Japan and a solo exhibition at Bodhi in London. The artist's oeuvre of brash, bold strokes, often of female faces,
has led to numerous live painting events in London, including at street festivals, bars and galleries. In 2008,
Nao partook in a painter's colony in Bosnia. Nao is represented by agent Gillen in New York and most recently
released products in collaboration with And A.

judit
garcia
talavera

Judit García-Talavera was always surrounded by beauty in her birthplace of Spain's Canary Islands. After graduating with a degree in fine arts at the Universidad de La Laguna, she sought to proliferate that beauty to all around her. Now the Barcelona-based artist produces illustrations featuring beautiful flowing lines that are the hallmark of her work. She adores the fountain pen and often finds herself combining ink and diluted watercolors to depict characters absorbed by their emotions or lost deep in daydreams.

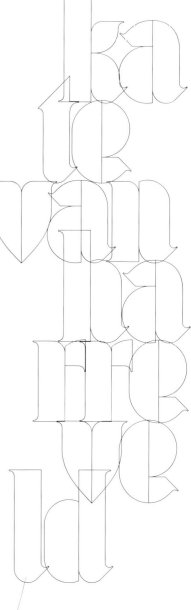

DAISY
MARC JACOBS

natalie
brockett

Artist Natalie Brockett graduated from the Queensland College of Art in Brisbane. She enjoyed a plum gig at a prestigious
studio before deciding to leave the Australian shores for hectic Tokyo. Inspired by an eclectic range of sources,
including vintage ephemera, fashion, and nature, Brockett now divides her time between graphic design and illustration.
Her work can be characterized as intuitive and experimental, varying from painstakingly detailed depictions,
vivid color, and structured compositions to more carefree approaches – scribbles in black and white, loose
pen and ink drawings, and mixed media collages.

linn olofsdotter

1. PREDATOR, 2006. Print – Fireroof. 2. SURREAL, 2009. Editorial – Tian. 3. ALEXANDER MCQUEEN, 2010. Retail – Plaza Magazine. 4. STUFFCATTERPL, 2009. Advertising – Storequeen.com. 5. EASTER WITCH, 2009. Self promotion – Fireroof.

Illustrator Linn Olofsdotter originally hails from Sweden but is now based in Portland, Oregon. Her art is an ocean of romantic stories strung together to form a tapestry of collected textures, drawings, and explosive colors with a hint of the surreal and naughty.

1. EXTRA LARGE - DIVE, 2009 · Exhibition - Catalog
2. ADVANCED MIXED JET 2010 · Edition - Huta Marianne
3. < 10 JET 2007 · Kaselowsky - Kaselowsky
4. HF · IF · 2009 · Eureka

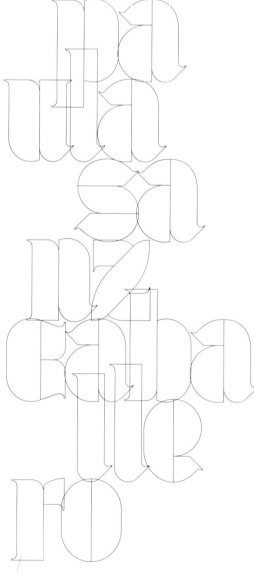

paula sanz caballero

Using science as a starting point, Spanish artist Paula Sanz Caballero shows special interest in the human figure. She is highly concerned with anatomy, which she has studied in depth, as well as the movement of the body and its way of expressing itself. Depending on what she wants to express in each piece, or on the composition, she reduces the elements to their most basic lines without losing realism. Before a sophisticated and luxurious backdrop, her stories tell us about the most primary of human feelings.

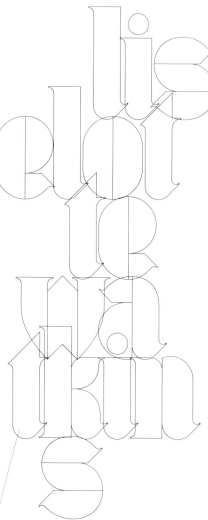

liselotte watkins

Liselotte Watkins, born in 1971, attended the Art Institute of Dallas and launched her career as an illustrator in New York. Her unique style garnered immediate attention and she landed the prestigious assignment to illustrate Barneys makeup advertisement every Sunday in the New York Times. Today Liselotte works with many of the biggest clients, including The New Yorker, Vogue, Elle, H&M, Miu Miu, Net-a-porter, MAC Cosmetics, Sephora, and Anna Sui. She works out of Milan and Stockholm and has published two books Watkin's Heroine and Watkin's Box of Pin-ups, which will soon be followed by Watkin's No 1.

1. DOROTHEA, 2010, Editorial – Elle. 2. FILIPPA, 2008, Exhibition – Fiancee. 3. DOROTHEA, 2010, Editorial – Elle. 4. BALENCIAGA, 2009, Editorial – Elle. 5. COVER INTERPRETATION, 2010, Editorial – D Magazine/La Repubblica. 5. DOROTHEA, 2010, Editorial – Elle.

olka osadzinska

Artist Olka Osadzinska may be young, but she has already whittled her sharps with big name brands such as Max Factor, Hugo Boss, Paramount Pictures, Nike, and Jägermeister. Based in Warsaw, Poland, she has worked with several Polish fashion and lifestyle magazines including Glamour, Machina, and Warsaw Insider. Her interest in fashion has led to collaborations with clothing brands like PROSTO (a Polish hip hop brand), Steve Aoki's DIM MAK Collection, and Polish pop singer Reni Jusis as part of an anti-HIV AIDS campaign.

1. LEFT ILLUSTRATION, MAX Beauty at Max Factor Club, illustration for Max Factor, September 2 RIGHT ILLUSTRATION, Max Factor, September 3 EYEBUSTER, 2009, advertisement, Yamaha Impact, 11 March 2009 4 LP cover illustration, Reni Jusis, 5 LOVE CAGE, 2010, advertisement

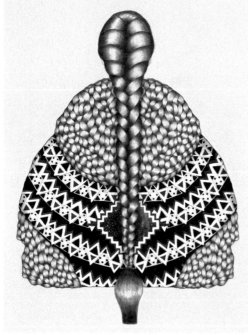

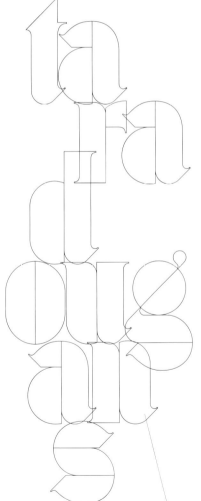

Tara Dougans is a Canadian designer and illustrator whose work is heavily influenced by the virtue of "taking one's time." Feeling that the value of process is often undermined by that of expediency, Dougans indulges her work with the luxury of time, focusing specifically on handcraftsmanship, and detail-oriented design.

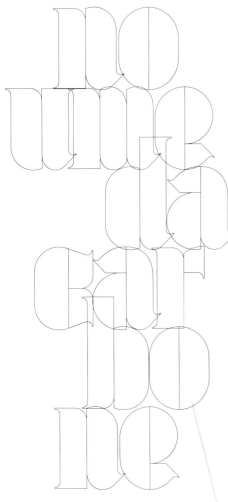

1. TOKYO KITSCH, SALON 01, 2009. Advertisement – Fashion front cover, manufacturer. 2. VODAFIRMA 85/1, 2009. Advertisement – Kitt immagine. 3. 30x ROME MAXXMI, MAXISSEX'S, 2010. Illustration/t, exhibit exhibit/tee (formation created. 4. FLUFF 2010, pin 010, 2008, pin 2010, Advertisement – contemporary advertisement created. 5. SIX/LUXE INTERIOR, MASTER, 05, 2009. Advertisement – Fashion advertisement, created.

Born in Paris, based in Florence, Noumeda Carbone works with a variety of tools – ink, pigment liner, felt-tip pen – to create perfectly imperfect hand drawings before glossing them over with digital instruments. She likes errors, the small surprises between lines, and the light. The freelance illustrator and painter has been included in a large number of publications, including Rolling Stone, Kult, Nylon, La Perla, 200 Best Illustrators Worldwide, Illusive 2, the Guardian, and more.

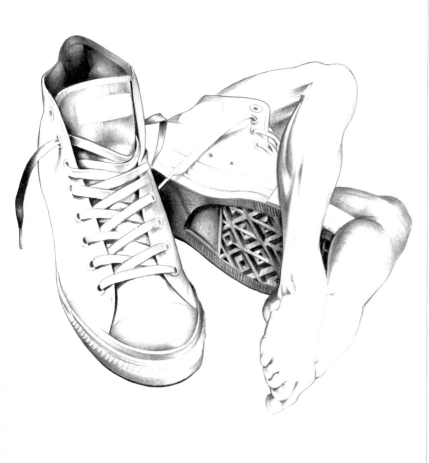

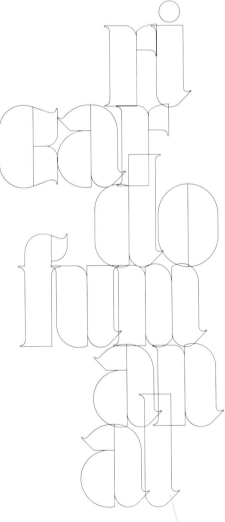

ricardo fumanal

Born in Huesca in 1984 and now based in London, Ricardo Fumanal first got his training at
the Lleida Secondary School of Arts, then later working for publications such as Dazed & Confused,
German Glamour, El País/EP3, Wallpaper* and Nylon Guys. He is currently interested in
photography for fashion and expanding from the realm of manual drawing (marker, pencil and
ink on paper) into moving images. His compositional identity is defined by simplicity and a
confrontation between figures and background.

pierretouismascia

1./2./4. STYLESCOPE, 2010 Editorial – Vogue US
3. BALENCIAGA, 2007 Editorial – Madriz
5./6. UNTITLED, 2009 Advertising – Première Classe
7. GUCCI, 2007 Editorial – Madriz
8. MC QUEEN, 2007 Editorial – Madriz

Dutch illustrator Piet Paris is a highly lauded illustrator, having been the creative vision behind a Saks Fifth Avenue campaign in 2009 and the man behind the eponymous product design studio. His sharply geometric illustrations play with retro elements, 3-D design and cut out imagery. He graduated from the Academy of Fine Arts in Arnhem in 1998 and is a co-founder of the Fashion Institute in Arnhem.

1. RED LIGHT FASHION, 2008 -Advertising - City of Amsterdam 2. CIRCLE, TRIANGLE, SQUARE, 2007 -Advertising – Bijenkorf Department Store 3. BANGLES, 2008 -Advertising – Saks Fifth Avenue 4. TWINS, 2008 -Advertising – W Korea 5. XL RED, 2008 -Advertising – W Korea

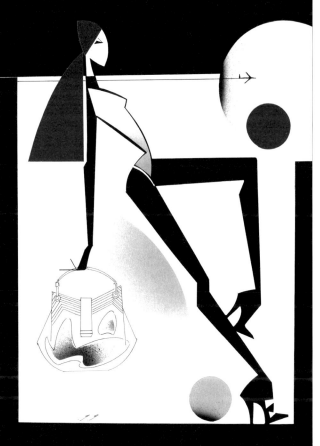

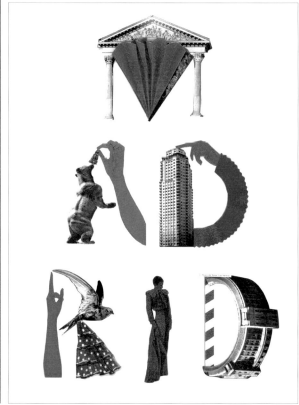
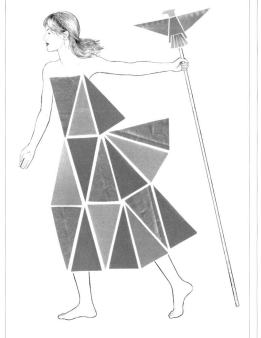
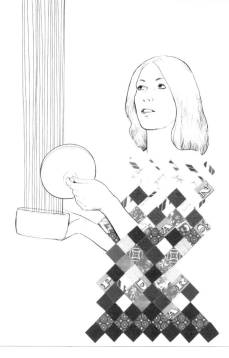

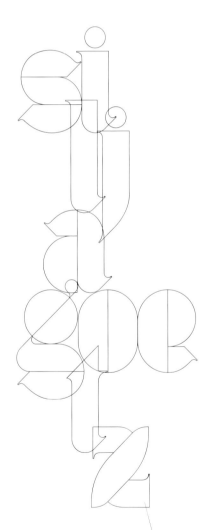

German-born illustrator Silja Goetz now works in Madrid, Spain. Before becoming a full-time freelancer,
she worked for two years as graphic designer for Allegra Magazine in Hamburg. Her long list of
clients include The New Yorker, El País, Nylon, Vogue, Nike, New York Magazine, Kiehl's, and the Bill
Clinton Foundation. She is represented by Art Department in New York.

james dignan

1. CAPRICORN, 2007, Editorial – Elegance. 2. DITA VON TEESE, 2009, "Be Cointreauversial" blog, Pendulum Tokyo – Cointreau. 3. EMMANUELLE BEART, 2007, Editorial "Festival de Cannes" – Madame Figaro. 4. ACATRIN-DESIGN, 2010, Invitation card – Acatrin-Design. 5. SARAH JESSICA PARKER, 2008, Editorial – Madame Figaro. 6. SARAH JESSICA PARKER, 2008, Editorial – Madame Figaro. 7. CHRISTIAN LOUBOUTIN, 2009, Editorial – Vogue Australia.

New Zealand-born James Dignan graduated in fashion, textile print design, and fashion illustration from the Berçot in Paris. Since 1990, Dignan's fashion and editorial illustrations have appeared in international publications including Vogue Australia, Glamour, The New Yorker, InStyle, the New York Times, the Los Angeles Times, Esquire, and Visonaire. Dignan has participated in numerous advertising campaigns and his work has adorned book covers, clothing, busses, and billboards. He currently lives and works in Sydney.

fashion note
no. 233
Max Mara

fashion note
no. 224
Burberry Prorsum

fashion note
no. 226
Alexander Wang

fashion note
no. 222
Marc by
Marc Jacobs

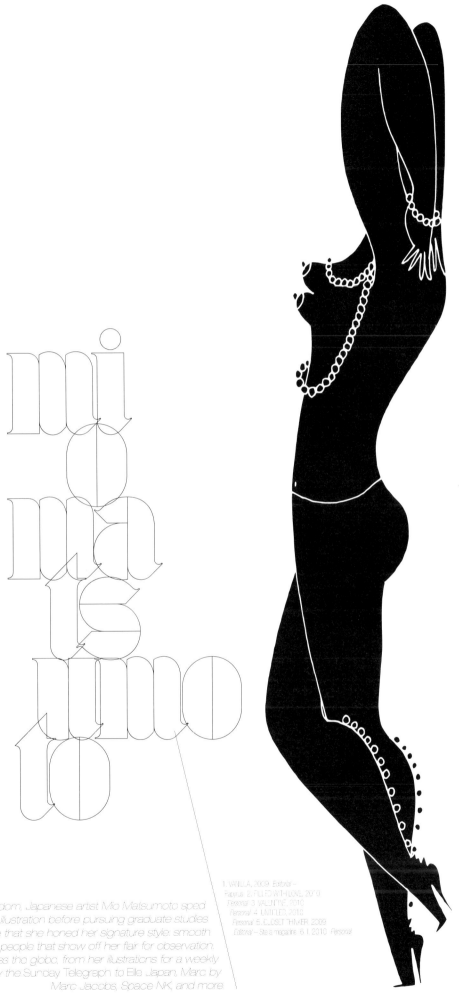

mio matsumoto

With her sights set on studying in the United Kingdom, Japanese artist Mio Matsumoto sped through Kingston University with a degree in illustration before pursuing graduate studies at the Royal College of Art. It was during this time that she honed her signature style, smooth pen portraits of everyday life and ordinary people that show off her flair for observation. Nowadays, Matsumoto's work can be seen across the globe, from her illustrations for a weekly fashion column in Stella Magazine by the Sunday Telegraph to Elle Japan, Marc by Marc Jacobs, Space NK, and more.

1. VANILLA, 2009. *Editorial –
Fabrics* 2. FILLED WITH LOVE, 2010.
Personal 3. VALENTINE, 2010.
Personal 4. UNTITLED, 2010.
Personal 5. CLOSET THIEVER, 2009.
Editorial – Stella magazine 6. I, 2010. *Personal*

Tal Drori is an illustrator, interaction designer, and graphic designer. She is based in Milan, where she works as a consultant and teaches design. Her work has been exhibited and published worldwide. Her clients and projects include: the Triennale Milano, Ozone Tokyo, the Israel Museum in Jerusalem, Domus magazine, and Fashioning the Future, published by Ed. Thames & Hudson. She holds a bachelor's degree in visual communication design from the Bezalel Academy of Art and Design in Jerusalem and a master's degree in interaction design from the Interaction Design Institute in Ivrea.

1. WONDER, 2010. Personal 2. LOTTA, 2010. Personal 3. BOY IN BOOT 2010 1. LOTTA, 2010. Personal 4. FLOWERS & STRIPES DRESS, 2009. Personal RED JACKET, 2009. Personal 6. DOTS, 2006. Personal

Victoria Boysen

Victoria Boysen has been drawing ever since she could hold a pen in her hand. Living by the
age-old adage that practice makes perfect, Boysen still considers herself a work in progress. For her,
being an illustrator is a parallel life, not her main occupation; it is a way for her to buoy
boredom and reach satisfaction. Boysen experiments using different techniques – sometimes
using just a pencil or ink to enhance dark areas, other times making watercolor
pigments her best friend.

1. MINIVADAROCCHIO, Personal 2. THE UNDRINKER,
2009, Personal 3. THE SWEATER, 2009, Personal
4. PANTOMME, PART 1, 2009, Personal 5. MMM, 2009, Personal
6. REDHEAD, 2009, Personal

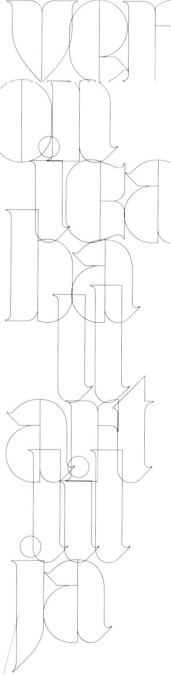

veronica ballart llija

Skönhet

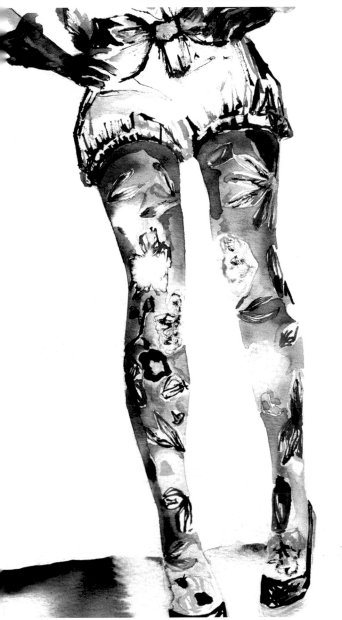

Graphic designer, product designer, and illustrator Tess Jacobson is the brains behind the self-named Tess J Design. The studio creates visual expressions for clients through graphic design and illustrations. Solutions are tailor-made and built upon close interaction with clients as all individual projects' needs a unique solution. The goal is to create design that is sustainable and that both parties are proud of.

1. FORESTLADY, 2008. *Personal* 2. PINKLADY, 2008. *Personal* 3. CIRCUSLADY, 2008. *Personal* 4. TOPPHALSA, 2010. *Editorial – Bonniers veckotidningar* 5. ACCESSORIES, 2008. *Editorial – Agenturföretagen* 6. PINKLADY, 2008. *Personal*

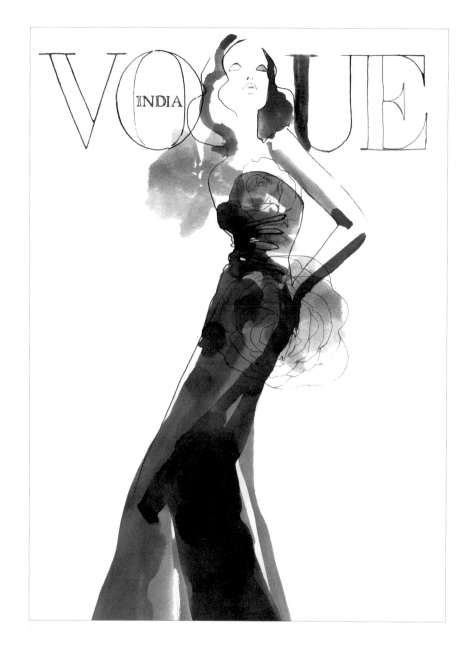

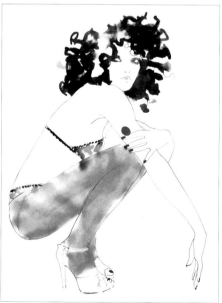

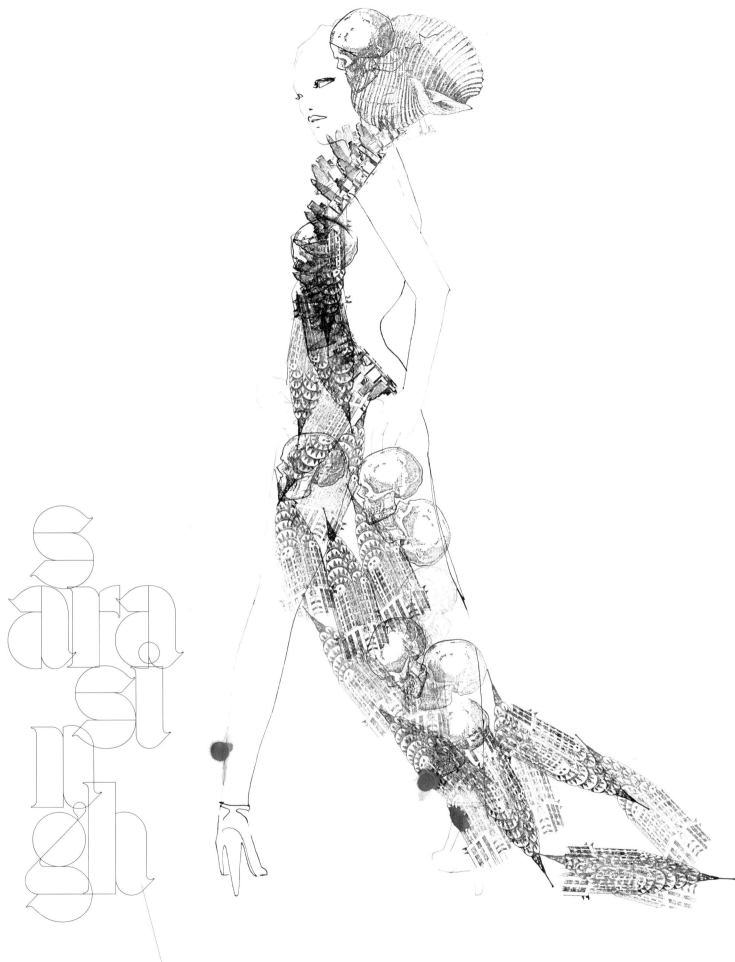

sara singh

1. VOGUE INDIA 2010 *Editorial – Vogue India*
LOOKING GLASS VOGUE 2007 *Personal* 3. URBS 2110 *Editorial*
MAGU U/S 4. SILICONE 2009 *Personal – Exhibition* 5. PERFUME
2008 *Editorial – Vogue Nippon* 6. MANHATTAN PROJECT *Exhibition*

Dividing her time between New York's Lower East Side and Stockholm,
artist and filmmaker Sara Singh declares cities as her main source of inspiration.
She has had solo exhibitions in Paris, Tokyo, and New York.

1. CORSET 2007 *Personal* – *Exhibition* 2. ANAÏS NIN, 2010 *Personal* –
Book cover 3. AFRO, 2007 *Personal* – *Exhibition* 4. SAYING CLEVER, 2007
Personal – *Exhibition* 5. ASCOT, 2010 *Personal* 6. TURBO DRESS 1, 2009
Advertising – *Estée Lauder* 7. TURBO DRESS 2007 *Advertising* – *Estée Lauder*
8. POWDER PUFF 2007 *Exhibition* 9. LIPSTICK 2010 *Editorial* – *Glamour USA*

The Diary of
Anaïs Nin
Volume 1
1931 – 1934

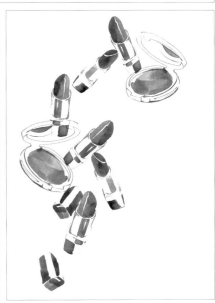

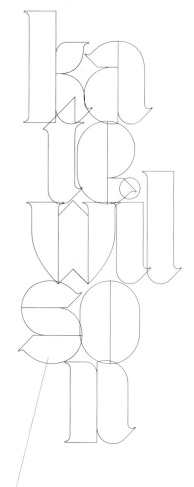

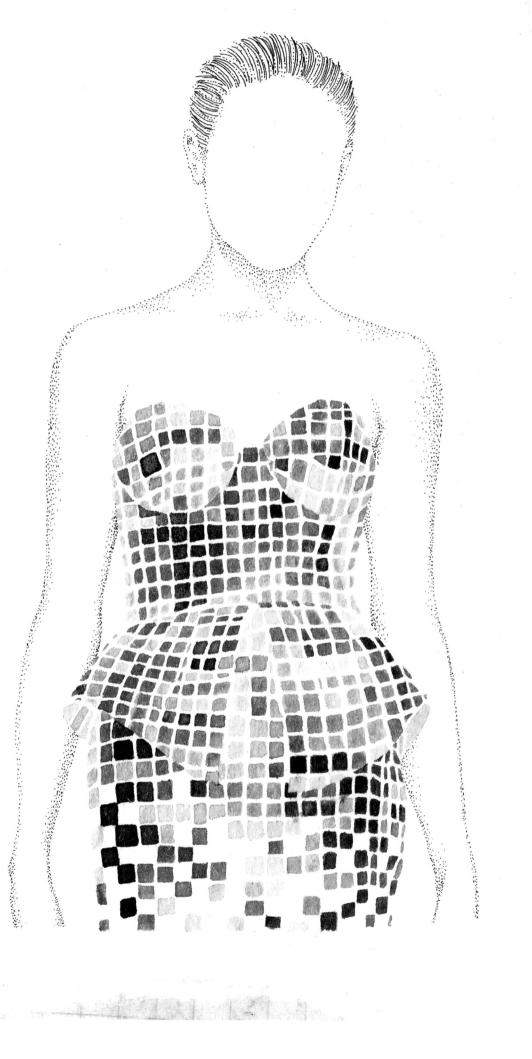

1 / 2 / 3 / 4 / 5 PERSONA SKETCHBOOK WORLD 20.09.2010 Fiona Shellrock

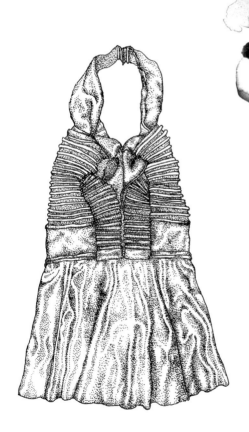

leather dress
christopher kane

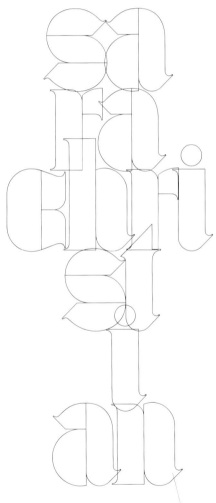

Sara Christian's ethereal paintings explore how people communicate through fashion – from beauty regimes to traditional costume. Her characters emerge from a spontaneous and layered process. She uses a variety of materials, inspired by textures and patterns from urban decay and consumer waste.

kareem iliya

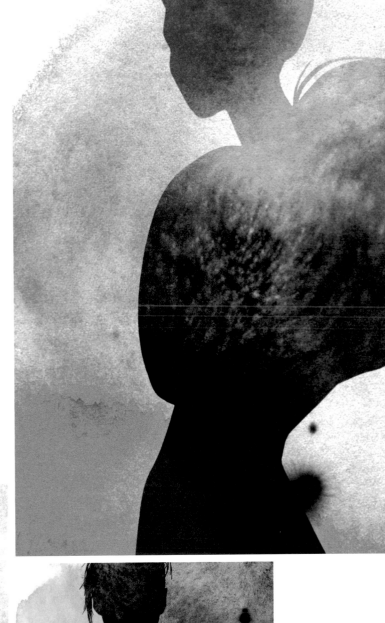

the beautiful

ILLUSTRATIONS FOR FASHION AND STYLE

The Beautiful
Illustrations for Fashion and Style

Edited by Anneke Krull, Robert Klanten and Hendrik Hellige
Texts by Youyoung Lee

Cover layout by Hendrik Hellige for Gestalten
Cover illustration by Lulu*
Layout by Hendrik Hellige for Gestalten
Typefaces: Ogaki by Áron Jancso, Foundry: www.gestalten.com/fonts;
Neue Helvetica, Foundry: Linotype

Project management by Elisabeth Honerla for Gestalten
Production management by Martin Bretschneider for Gestalten
Proofreading by Rebecca Silus
Printed by Offsetdruckerei Grammlich GmbH, Pliezhausen
Made in Germany

Published by Gestalten, Berlin 2010
ISBN 978-3-89955-321-5

© Die Gestalten Verlag GmbH & Co. KG, Berlin 2010

Bibliographic information published by the Deutsche Nationalbibliothek.
The Deutsche Nationalbibliothek lists this publication in the Deutsche Nationalbibliografie;
detailed bibliographic data is available online at http://dnb.d-nb.de.

None of the content in this book was published in exchange for payment by commercial parties or designers;
Gestalten selected all included work based solely on its artistic merit.

This book was printed according to the internationally accepted FSC standards for environmental
protection, which specify requirements for an environmental management system.

Mixed Sources
Product group from well-managed
forests and other controlled sources
www.fsc.org Cert no. IMO-COC-028001
© 1996 Forest Stewardship Council

Gestalten is a climate-neutral company and so are our products. We collaborate with the non-profit carbon offset provider
myclimate (www.myclimate.org) to neutralize the company's carbon footprint produced through our worldwide business
activities by investing in projects that reduce CO$_2$ emissions (www.gestalten.com/myclimate).